D0974260

Dead Stuck

By Richard Mounce, DDS

Dead Stuck
By Richard Mounce, DDS
Copyright ©2009 by Richard Mounce

All rights reserved. No part of this publication may be reproduced or transmitted in any form or by any means, electronic or mechanical, including photocopy, recording, or any information storage and retrieval system, without permission in writing from the publisher.

Copyright ©2009
Pacific Sky Publishing
Vancouver, WA 98684

Library of Congress Cataloging-in-Publication Data
Mounce, Richard
Dead Stuck/Richard Mounce

ISBN 978-0-615-33011-2
2009939698
Printed in the United States of America
First edition 2009

Cover Photo by Paul Heinerth ©2009. This image of the author was taken in the Devil's Eye cave entrance of the Little Devil's Cave system, Ginnie Springs, Florida.

This book is dedicated to my wife, Laura, and twin daughters, Alana and Bianca. All my love, I am still in awe.

Special thanks to: Emily Schauer, Fiona Collins, Kirsten Komara, Bob Gannon, Fred Michmershuizen, Houda Naayem, Lisa Moler, Lynne Smith, Mick Hoban, Libby Gill, Dennis Ghormley, George Mounce III, Penny Mounce, Tim Smith, Tim Chapman, Steve Bogaerts, Brian Kakuk, Theresa Kohlhoff, Brian Hollander, Ed O'Mara, Warren Mersereau, Sergio Rosler, Shawn Potter, Paul Heinerth, Ghia Sarouphim, Marcel Hagendijk, Courtney Willis, Anna Friedhoff, Phillip Barrett, J. Mauricio Giraldo, Gary Glassman, Lauren Bundschuh, Thomas Iliffe, Sean Seaberg, Dave Monette, Agnes Milowka, Philip Porter, Ricardo V. Rodriguez, Joe Kieffer, Julian English, Howard Carsman, James Kangas, John Weever, Gary Glassman, Laura, Alana and Bianca.

Contents

Part 1 Armchair Adventures and Miracles   11
    1) E-Mails From the Road   12
    2) Dead Stuck at 123 Feet Underwater   18
    3) Fear. The Spice of Life   28
    4) Football Addiction and the Miracle at Highbury   33
    5) Man Wears Girl Repellant   42

Part 2 Setting the Kids Free   55
    A Christmas Letter to Remember   56

Part 3 Marriage: "Come to Heal"   83
    1) Marry Her When   84
    2) Finding "The One"   93
    3) For Men   101
    4) For Women   105
    5) Should I Stay or Should I Go?   108
    6) And Finally   114

Epilogue   118
Appendix A: Q&A: "The Overhead Environment"   120
Appendix B: References   129
Appendix C: Endnotes   138

Preface

"Teachers of Literature are apt to think up such problems as "What is the author's purpose?" or still worse "What is the guy trying to say?" Now, I happen to be the kind of author who in starting to work on a book has no other purpose than to get rid of that book and who, when asked to explain its origin and growth, has to rely on such ancient terms as Interreaction of Inspiration and Combination-which, I admit, sounds like a conjurer explaining one trick by performing another." (Nabokov 311)

Dead Stuck boisterously describes how being a root canal specialist (endodontist) has provided me unique opportunities and challenges in marital and parental relationships, how I once wore girl repellent, my addiction to world football, diverted flights with fire on the wing and mortal danger encountered while cave diving.

I do not believe this book is not courageous in its disclosure. Its always been my bias that if people were honest with themselves and those around them that they would be happier, especially when the truth is not pretty. I wrote *Dead Stuck* to speak my truth on a number of subjects without hiding behind politically correct clichés and platitudes. The lengthy period from its conception to birth gives evidence to a nagging doubt that if I lifted my skirt and made this public, it just might be ugly! Ugly or not, this child is born and my hope is that sharing the contents of *Dead Stuck* will resonate with those who can see themselves in some part of its varied subject matter.

The experiences related in the chapters of Part 3 (Marriage: "Come to Heal") are a semi autobiographical personal memoir. Some of this material is my personal history and much of it is not. The conclusions I draw in these chapters are my truth. It is up to the reader to decide what they believe and want for themselves. I have no intention to preach or tell the reader what they should do. I intentionally chose the language and tone of these chapters to provoke thought, dialogue and reflection.

What constitutes a marriage for one person or couple may be entirely different from another. Varying definitions of marriage bring varying goals, expectations and desired behavior, all of which may be contrary to mine. I write of marriage in the traditional manner of two people coming together with the intention to remain mated as monogamous partners for life. There are many routes to a destination, in this case a happy and fulfilling long-term marriage. What is written describes my path. I encourage the reader to compare notes as they walk on theirs in dating and marriage.

A special note of thanks goes out to Fred Michmershuizen, my editor. His suggestions and reflections were an invaluable resource.

I take personal responsibility for all errors within, factual, philosophical or otherwise. I write of God with the male pronoun. I could have called God "She" or "Her" and it would have been every bit as valid.

Blessings, Peace, Love and Light,

Richard Mounce, DDS
Vancouver, Washington, USA
October 2009

Part 1

Armchair Adventures and Miracles

Chapter 1

E-Mails From the Road

"Own only what you can carry with you; know language, know countries, know people. Let your memory be your travel bag." (McHugh 38)

Alexander Solzhenitsyn (1918 – 2008) (Alexander Solzhenitsyn dies at 89)

I am a root canal specialist (endodontist) by profession. In addition to having a full time private practice, I write and travel globally, teaching in my specialty. Lecturing in over 30 countries, in addition to providing free dentistry for the needy in four others has profoundly altered my worldview. My time out of the office has been rewarding, enlightening and sobering. It has reinforced to me how blessed I am.

For example, while lecturing in Cambodia, a dentist told me, as a young boy, how thugs from the Khmer Rouge put a gun to his head and voted on whether he should be shot on sight for allowing a cow to momentarily escape his attention. In Qatar, I had tea with a very polite dentist who, with a straight face, explained why she believed Israel should be annihilated. Paradoxically, some of the most genuine warmth and hospitality I have experienced as a traveler and teacher has been in the Middle East. On my lecture travels, I've explained the American invasion of Iraq to befuddled Japanese in Sapporo and been told in Buenos Aires of the struggle of farmers facing the prospect of new taxes under the presidency of Cristina Fernández de Kirchner (Cristina Fernández de Kirchner). *I have had aspects of Hindu spiritual practice described to me in Madrid while having lunch at the Santiago Bernabéu, the home of Real Madrid football club. In Russia, I've survived extravagant toasts that continued for hours, been encouraged to shoot vodka before speaking and been obligated to kiss mobsters on the cheek.*

In Riyadh, Saudi Arabia, during the five daily prayers (ṣalāt), the stores close, adding in some small measure to what is already monumental traffic. It was during one of these traffic jams at midday that I had a deeply personal conversation with a Palestinian dentist whose father was an immigrant to Saudi Arabia. Even though born in Saudi Arabia and living there since birth, this man will never be able to become a Saudi citizen, as he cannot obtain a Saudi passport. His wife and children also cannot have Saudi passports. In essence, this man and his family have no country of their own. In sweltering heat, driving around Riyadh in circles, we discussed Islam, Israel, 9/11 and the prospects for peace in the Middle East. The conversation left an impression on us both. We became friends and remain in touch. Among many tough questions, I asked him, "If you were the American president, what would you have done on September 12, 2001?" He had a few tough questions for me in return. Our differing nationalities and religions evaporated. We were two men from completely different worlds communicating as human beings without filters or pretense, an experience I would not trade for anything.

I was on the River Neva in St. Petersburg, Russia late one evening on a cruise boat as part of a formal dinner connected with a dental conference. Due to the "Midnight Sun," it was still relatively light late in the evening as we floated along. My friend was chatting with a knockout female Russian dentist seated at a table across the boat. My host told me that the dentist with whom my friend was intimately speaking was actually the mistress of a local mafioso. This man was purportedly plying the woman with clothes, a car, a house and money for both her and her family in exchange for sexual exclusivity. Pressing to find out who the man was, my host adamantly refused to tell me, leading me to believe with certainty that the individual was on the boat and watching my friend chatting up his hired paramour. Hoping to signal my buddy with the throat cutting hand gesture from across the boat and mouth the word "ixnay" on flirting with this dangerous liaison, I was unable to get his attention. Doing my best 007, I moved nonchalantly in their direction to warn him and try not to get us both killed in the process. I believed the threat was real. While the woman in question was clearly intrigued by my friend, he told me later that she never crossed a line of formality in their conversation so as to not run afoul of her keeper. Fortunately, neither of us ended up with concrete shoes as fish food at the river's bottom.

In the middle of a lecture in Dubai, an Egyptian professor unexpectedly stood up and began to protest at the top of his voice. My first reaction was that he intended to take us both to the Promised Land. My sphincter tightened when I saw him rise up shouting words I did not immediately comprehend. We parted with a handshake and a smile upon speaking at the presentation's conclusion.

I've taken away cell phones from doctors having live conversations while sitting in Row 1. A skirt, slit deliberately to the hip, has revealed a garter belt intending to make an impression from Row 2. Rhythmic belching on the quarter hour has serenaded me from Row 3. I've had to stop a doctor flashing pictures of my lecture that were momentarily blinding me from Row 4. A man from Row 5 once followed me into the bathroom to argue his clinical opinions while I was answering nature's call. Such is the life of an endodontist who lectures and travels globally. Who says root canals are boring?

The following travel stories were written on the road and sent to friends and family by e-mail. These e-mails appear much as they did when originally sent.

Travel Story #1:

Dear Alana and Bianca,

Hola...here's a story you can't tell every day!

It was a hell of a day in NY Friday...long story short, red eye to Newark Thursday night, town car to LaGuardia (did a hands on course[1] there, all went well), flew to Boston, flight was diverted due to engine trouble on the left wing, some passengers said they saw fire on the left engine, the engine clearly didn't sound right, the plane didn't feel right, one lady was shrieking a bit...my heart raced initially but from my cave diving...you aren't dead until your dead, no balls/no babies...and all that...you could hear a pin drop in the plane as we diverted to Hartford and landed safely (Praise God!), taxi to Boston ($300), was almost immediately backstage standing next to Sting and Yo Yo Ma before they went on during a Chris Botti PBS concert with the Boston symphony (the show included John Mayer, Steven Tyler, and many other talented people), the music was truly world class...and during the middle of the show this poor guy has a heart attack two seats over from Laura in the 4th row (no pulse, etc), stopped the show for 30 minutes, etc...he was revived! Sting, Yo Yo Ma and Chris Botti played a moving rendition of the song "Fragile" to ease the audience back into the concert... its a long story how we got separated and didn't sit together while this was going on....I got 3 hours sleep out to NY (Thursday p.m.) and 3 hours sleep last night (Friday p.m.) I am now on the flight back home Saturday morning. I'll arrive home at about 11 a.m. this morning and we have 12 people coming for dinner tonight at the house at 6 p.m.! I have a friend and patient (great guy) who makes custom trumpets for the best players in the world, he got the "all access" passes to get me (and Laura) back stage during and after the show...phuk!

Quite a day I/we won't forget... A lifetime memory.... Rich

P.S.: I can't sleep...am writing endo articles...dad loves you both very much...we are all truly blessed...use your gifts, find your passion, and work very hard, never stop trying.

Travel Story #2

I am sorry for the radio silence during this trip...it has been the fastest pace of the trips I've done abroad...there has been very little down time...

Anyway, on a lighter note I am going to tell you what happened in a very short version trying to get from Athens to Riyadh...I misconnected in Bahrain...i.e. we were late out of Athens and I missed the flight to Riyadh by no more than 5 minutes. After waiting for 90+ minutes in a lounge I was told they had found me a hotel and I go and get in a van with other unfortunate travelers who shared the same fate. We drive to the hotel (20 minutes) and get out only to be told that a mistake had been made and that we had to drive back to the airport to let Gulf Air sort it out again to get us rooms somewhere else. After 15 minutes of haggling, it turns out that there are indeed 2 rooms available. I get one. Upon entering it, I find its not been cleaned, beds are stripped, dirty towels on the bathroom floor, etc. I ask for fresh towels and after 20 minutes they send a very well groomed gentleman from Pakistan who speaks minimal English but embodies the expression "Smile and the world smiles back at you," think big teeth, slick hair...who upon seeing the room immediately says "You did this." After trying to explain that I found the room like this with hand gestures and explaining that I only wanted clean towels, he comes back 20 minutes later with bed sheets (when I only asked for towels) and wants to make up the room (he also brought some towels in fairness to him)...despite the fact that I keep asking him to leave, he didn't seem to understand or want to leave, it was surreal. Anyway, he finally did and we parted the best of friends. This hotel was loaded with Russian working girls servicing foreign guys, impossible to miss. You can scratch the Days Hotel in Bahrain off your properties of the world list of must see "boutique" hotspots.

I was going to miss my morning lecture in Riyadh because of the "misconnect." When the guys at the company found out about the misconnect, the local dealer in Saudi got a driver for me who was supposed to take me to Riyadh by car, leaving immediately. It's now 10:30 p.m. Riyadh is 400 km from Bahrain (275 miles ish). So I go downstairs to check out and the man at the front desk won't give me my passport back. It's complex, but he claimed that he had the right to keep the passport for x, y, z reasons and I stopped my uncontrollable urge to reach across the desk and throttle the bastard. You had to be there because the blow by blow of this was really tragically funny (me being held semi captive by a guy who I knew was wrong, having so few good options, knowing that getting angry was strictly out of the question, intuitively knowing this guy was just pulling my chain, yada yada)...When the dealer in Saudi found out what was happening, he literally woke up the president of the Bahrain dental society who called his friend, who was in the local police force. After about 8 phone calls and I am sure threats of a police action, an uprising and other such nonsense, my passport was returned with a smile by the same guy who held it with a smirk. Now it is 12:30 a.m. and I meet Samir, an indentured servant from India who was to be my driver.

We head to the Saudi border where I am fingerprinted and photographed because I am the son of George and Mickey and come from the land of the free and the home of the brave. Off we go...only issue is that Samir has an audible alarm that goes off whenever the car is above 120 km/hour. For the entire night, driving across the Saudi desert (and I mean flatter than a pancake, nothing, brown dirt, worse than North Dakota at its worst, really flat) passing the oil rigs/facilities including the kind that shoot flames in the air. I am serenaded in my completely broken sleep with a very audible "ching ching" speed alarm, all of this in the interest of better root canals for all.

Then, mid ride, I got to pee! Back teeth are floating, big time pee... but Samir keeps driving after I've told him twice we need to stop...now its full tilt, desperation, injury time[2] got to pee, finally, by the grace of the good Lord we find a roadside gas station in the middle of BFE (except its BF Saudi) and all was made well again. At 5:15 a.m. we arrived in Riyadh. Now I am completely wired, slept relatively little in the car (think almost 5 hours of ching ching-sounds like a viable truth serum strategy) and am facing a whole day of lecturing, starting at 9 a.m., which I did, if I might say so, with great aplomb. So there you have it...I am really looking forward to coming home to my wonderful wife and the relative peace of Vancouver, Washington...

This scratches the surface of this trip...there is much, much, more, love to all.

Chapter 2

Dead Stuck at 123 Feet Underwater

"Life is either a daring adventure or nothing. Security does not exist in nature, nor does the children of men as a whole experience it. Avoiding danger is no safer in the long run than exposure." (Kumar 217)

Helen Keller (1880 – 1968) (The Life of Hellen Keller)

It is one thing for people outside the profession to talk about dentistry in the abstract without any real understanding of the stresses that come with the occupation. It is entirely different to be the clinician working to produce a positive result with an anxious or uncooperative patient. Being graceful under pressure is harder than it looks.

Dental school is a marathon, not a sprint. After college, it takes grit to stay in school for an additional four years to earn a dental degree and then even more intestinal fortitude to sit for a clinical dental board treating live patients before being granted a license to practice.

Anxious as a "flunk out" practical examination loomed in dental school (Northwestern, Chicago), I had a revelation. Much was riding on this test. Failing meant having to repeat the class and possibly the academic year. The year before, a classmate of mine had been required to repeat his freshman year as a result of failing this same class. Grading is highly subjective in these practical examinations. The student is evaluated relative to a stylized replica model of an ideal cavity preparation, a process not unlike one artist judging another's sculpture. Gaining perspective as the practical grew near, I realized that up to that point in my education I had met every challenge put in my way. It gave me confidence that I could meet this one. I passed.

A residency of two to three years after dental school is required to become a certified endodontic specialist. Relatively few dental students go directly into residency programs; rather they usually have a few years of postgraduate clinical experience in the "real world" of one form or another. Residency is more of a job than "school." Grades are not generally emphasized in such programs. Residents tend to help one another, as competitive fire has usually given way to cooperation and peaceful coexistence. After residency, by the time endodontist hit the streets, they have been tested by fire. To one extent or another, they have had to produce acceptable results under adverse circumstances. Among a host of possible challenges, medical emergencies, wayward clinical results and difficult patients have had to be addressed. A person develops resilience with such training.

This resolve has served me well over the years. In 2003, considering a move to Hawaii, I flew seven people from Portland to Honolulu to take the Hawaii general dental board at my own expense. I housed, fed and transported these people to have primary patients and backup patients. The board consisted of a written exam, live patient procedures and bench top exercises. At that time, the state of Hawaii did not have licensure by credential (qualifying for a license by showing previous qualifications and licenses) nor did they have the specialty licenses that are common in some other states. Not having been a general dentist since 1988, I was required by the state of Hawaii to take a general dental board exam to prove my competency as an endodontic specialist. To gain eligibility to sit for the Hawaii examination, I was also required to take, for a second time, a written National Board examination (the National Board Part II) on basic clinical sciences that I had already passed as a dental student in 1984.

A general dental board is wholly irrelevant to endodontic clinical specialty practice. In my case, taking this examination was much like a cardiac surgeon being asked to take an OB/GYN examination to prove their skills in bypass surgery. I do not make the rules.

Coincident to this process, I experienced the only moment of my life where I have been racially abused. Having slept in approximately 60 countries in my travels, I still scratch my head that it happened in America by one of our own. It gave me empathy and a first hand look at racial politics. While detailing the incident is beyond the scope of Dead Stuck, I was unmistakably insulted for no other reason than being an outsider to deter my desire to gain a Hawaii license at a meeting of the Hawaii dental board. I had been invited by the board to speak on licensure by credential and traveled there at my own expense to do so. I swallowed hard and took the insult in stride while not showing a flicker of the volcanic anger that arose in me. I decided instantly, in that moment, I would never let this group of people either intimidate or discriminate against me. When confronted with the choice of giving up before the race began, or overcoming their arcane rules to obtain a Hawaiian license, there was little choice but to follow my dream and take them on by passing their board on their terms. Like The Little Engine That Could *in the story I used to read my girls at night, I believed I could do it.*

After passing the National Board Part II to become eligible to take the Hawaii general dental board, I spent almost every evening and weekend for the next six months practicing and relearning techniques that I had not done for the preceding 15 years. In direct cost and lost earnings the effort cost me approximately $60,000.

In the time frame that I took this board examination, the historical passing rates were approximately 40 to 55 percent. Preparing for the test, I spoke with numerous clinicians who had failed several times. A score of 3.00 out of 5.00 was required to pass. I scored a 3.02. This is as close as I will ever come to winning an Olympic gold medal, albeit in dentistry!

More importantly, among many such trials, it made it possible for me to believe that, with the help of God, I can handle life's challenges including getting dead stuck in the story that follows.

Beyond watching "Sea Hunt" as a kid in the 1960s and admiring Lloyd Bridges, I knew absolutely nothing about diving when I signed up for my first open water certification course in the summer of 2004. At that time I had no idea that there were underwater caves much less that someone might actually dive in them. But they do.

Cave divers, solo or in teams, are a different breed. On any given day, all over the world and especially in the Bahamas, Florida and the Yucatan Peninsula of Mexico, "cavers" are enthusiastically descending into the watery bowels of the earth (also known as the "overhead diving environment"). Caves have passages as small as the width of a body, or as large as Wrigley Field in Chicago. At the extreme end of the spectrum, hard-core cave divers live to connect cave systems and explore "virgin" (previously unexplored) caves with the fervor of religious zealotry. These people live near underwater caves and most often teach and guide other cave students and divers. Their days are spent in the water. Their nights are spent on Internet diving chats debating gear configurations, planning explorations, studying accident analysis and weighing in on site access controversies, among many other topical issues. Like others who are passionate about an activity, be it fishing, beer-in-the-butt chicken, dressage, knitting, cricket, softball, parcheesi, hang gliding or collecting smashed pennies, these divers want to be driving further and deeper into cave systems. They want to be "pushing cave." I've learned much from these passionate cave divers. They are my dive gurus, people I admire greatly for their skills, humility and passion.[3]

After my initial certifications, while reading about the Pacific Islands, I learned that it was possible to dive the shipwrecks of the 1954 Bikini Atoll nuclear tests. I discovered that the most comfortable divers on the wrecks in Bikini are cave divers. My dad served on the *USS Arkansas*, one of the warships sunk there. Having always wanted to touch one of my dad's ships, a quest was born, to dive the *USS Arkansas* and to leave a small memento of my mother on his ship as both my parents passed away years ago.

To become fully prepared for Bikini, I decided to get cave diving certified. Cave diving is an extreme sport and one that is worked up to. Divers rarely, if ever, start out anywhere near diving in caves. By the time divers might even consider cave diving, they would be expert open water divers and ideally have hundreds of dives under their belts. Only after significant training and certification would they be able to cave dive safely. This is a mountaintop that is earned, not one with a ski lift to the summit. My path to cave diving was no different. My dive certifications mushroomed. In less than four years, I became a Divemaster and went from cavern (entry level of the cave certification track) to full cave certified (the basic cave certification). Next came side mount cave diving. Side mount is an advanced form of cave diving where divers wear their gas cylinders under them instead of on their backs. Stage diving followed. Staging involves carrying additional cylinders into the cave, dropping them on the way in and picking them up on the exit. Stage diving allows much deeper cave penetrations. Other technical certifications, including diving with partial helium gas mixtures that include reduced amounts of oxygen and nitrogen (trimix), also became part of my underwater education.

Coexisting peacefully with my natural caution has been a growing zest for diving with each successive certification and positive experience. Part of my enthusiasm for cave diving is fueled by its complete tranquility. A cave underwater is so quiet that I can hear my dive partner breathing several feet away. The absence of sound and light is liberating. With less to distract me, my mind can focus wholly on the dive. Literally, with each foot further from the surface, my cares above water melt away when descending. It is an ironic duality. Facing a stark and unforgiving environment, I am freer than at any other time in my human experience. Cave diving uncouples my mind from objective reality. I become focused on only two purposes, to enjoy the serenity and stay alive. Nothing can touch me during the dive. I am out of reach of all of the pressures and stimuli that bombard me above the surface. Cave diving is as close to outer space as I can get without mind-altering substances or NASA. Everything that we call "life" in the waking hours above water disappears. For the period of the dive, the world becomes water, the cave and my air supply; it is very simple. To state that the experience is a small glimmer of being in the womb of one's mother would not miss the mark.

Some fear water. Some fear being in small spaces. I respect both. While I am not claustrophobic, drowning and especially in an enclosed space would not be my preferred method of dying. Having once nearly drowned while windsurfing on the Columbia River,[4] I can testify to the uncompromising nature of water when things go wrong. For me, water in any form is to be approached with the utmost seriousness. Details surrounding water are not to be left to chance. To this day even with the freedom I have found in cave diving, I am never entirely at ease while diving. I always plan for the worst.

Cave diving has a second "moth to the flame" attraction for me. I can be a true explorer. While I am not anywhere near the professional explorer class of cave diver, I have laid several hundred feet of virgin line with my dive guru at my heels orchestrating the proceedings. "Laura's Castle" is the name I gave to this section of cave in the Bahamas (The Abacos, Ralph's Cave), named after my wife. I can't say that I've ever had an original thought, but I will always look back fondly on the day that I first gazed on a portion of God's creation before any other human eyes.

Getting Dead Stuck

Knowing the limits to which we should push ourselves is a delicate balancing act. Cave diving or any activity involving physical risk, (such as rock or mountain climbing) at the highest level involves a series of ever more complex endeavors with an exponentially increasing risk of morbidity. In the end, one gets to the highest level, gives up or ends up dead in the pursuit of some perceived mountaintop. Is it worth it? Where should cave diving end for me? What is my Mt. Everest? Personally, this is a question for which, at this writing, I have no answer. However, I know with certainty that there is nothing in any cave worth dying for. Billy Deans, a fabled wreck diver, stated that "There are old divers, there are bold divers, but there are no old bold divers."(McMurray 106) I believe him. I am not invincible.

When asked by my wife on our first date what I wanted to do with my career and where I wanted it to end, I answered "To get to the mountaintop." Interestingly enough, looking me straight in the eye, her next question was, "What then?" I thought for a moment and replied, "Get down the mountain gracefully!" She smiled in an approving manner. Had I said, "Go find another mountain," I now know that I would have been left on the dust heap of other boys who wanted to be contenders in her life. My answer had shown that I cared not so much for peak bagging as much as trying to live with some semblance of proportion in a world that says that more is always better. At one point, if I recall correctly, the MTV motto was "Too much is never enough" which is akin to the philosophy "You can never be too rich or too thin." (Keyes 180) You can be both. Too much is more than needed.

In light of what follows, though you may not believe me, I would rather go cave diving with my dive gurus or solo cave by myself any day of the week. Either way, I would be much safer on an extended range cave dive than I would be on any open water dive boat, on any given day, in any tourist resort. While this sounds counterintuitive, I have had a dive boat come crashing down less than two feet from my head in heaving seas after entering to begin a recreational dive in Belize. I've seen divers taking pictures while simultaneously swimming backward toward propellers. In Palau, it is not unusual to see inexperienced divers literally carried underwater by guides to prevent them from making uncontrolled ascents. The day after Laura and I left Pelelui Island on a trip to Palau, a group of Asian divers went floating for hours when their dive boat could not find them after they ascended. Due to the legendary currents at Pelelui, they had surfaced away from their expected pickup point. Fortunately, the group drifted toward the nearest island (Anguar) and was found by their flashlight's glow as the darkness loomed. While recreational diving is generally very safe, the tales of open water dives gone wrong could fill many a book.

Many recreational dives are a "free for all." Divers with dissimilar equipment and varying training levels and experience from all over the world meet on a boat in dive resorts for the first time, buddy up and then jump in, often having to fend for themselves depending on the dive and the quality of the guide. In distinction, cave divers are trained to a much higher standard and have a rigid set of rules with regard to dive protocols, gear configurations and gas management. Dive plans are discussed and agreed upon among dive team members before descending. One dive is highly controlled and the other is generally not.

Give me the cave any day of the week. It doesn't move. The cave walls are a boundary, a limit, and a comforting safety. Most often, with cave diving, there is one way in and, all things being equal, one way out; a simple equation. There are fewer unknowns in cave diving than open water diving. The ground rules in this engagement are straightforward. The cave, while often stunningly beautiful, is trying to kill you. It tried to kill me.

At the time of getting dead stuck I was at the relative limit of my skill. The next progression in my cave diving education was to move through a small restriction, a body width passage from one cave "room" to the next. In side mount configuration, divers are more vertically compact compared to when wearing their tanks on their backs. This allows passage through smaller restrictions than would otherwise be possible wearing tanks on the divers' backs. To advance my skills, this restriction was a challenge I literally had to push through.

There are major restrictions, minor restrictions and a wide range in between. At one end of the spectrum, minor restrictions may require divers to alter their swimming posture or "trim" slightly but through which the divers should be able to pass uneventfully. Major restrictions require a number of advanced techniques that range from contorting your body to slither through the restriction, up to removing one or both tanks and pushing them in front of you. The goal is to become as small as possible in order to push and pull your body through the restriction until it is cleared. When absolutely necessary, some explorers "bong" their way forward if the restriction is so small that it cannot be traversed otherwise. While I have never done it, it has been explained to me that in certain situations it becomes necessary for divers to use their cylinders as a battering ram to break off (bong) small portions of rock that are restricting forward movement.

At the highest level of cave diving, explorers are taking almost all of their gear off and pushing their gas cylinders ahead of themselves through spaces that they can barely squeeze through and are doing so in virgin caves in zero visibility. When heading into such restrictions, explorers usually do not know if the cave is continuous with another larger space. Imagine pushing yourself underwater in an asymmetrical tube of rock surrounded on all sides that, after 15 to 20 feet, dead ends completely and then having to shimmy your way back out of the same space with fins on! You get the idea.

One legendary cave explorer in Mexico, Steve Bogaerts, had a cave system collapse on him in a fragile passage that blocked his exit. As a result, he could only go forward. The problem with forward was that he could not know if there was an exit ahead or if he could get to it without first running out of air. This man had balls of steel not to panic. Fortunately for him, there was an exit. With no water, no machete and only a general idea where his vehicle was, he had to fight his way out through the tropical bush in the heat of the day. While miserable and at risk for dehydration, this was far preferable to drowning.

As a novice on the advanced side of cave diving, without undue trepidation, I watched my dive guru move through a minor restriction, pushing one of his cylinders ahead of him. I was to follow. As I approached it, also pushing one of my tanks ahead of me, my first impression was that of a slam-dunk. My surge of confidence evaporated instantly. The restriction became rapidly smaller, as if I were watching videotape played at increasingly higher speeds. In the blink of an eye the ever-narrowing space closed around me. With each inch I pushed forward, the cave seemingly grew arms and grabbed me. I propelled myself forward using my knees, heels and elbows. All my exertions to gain linear inches in the restriction only more forcefully wedged me into the rock walls. Finally, I could not move. I was dead stuck 123 feet underwater. Not just dead stuck at 123 feet underwater, but at least 1,100 linear feet back in the cave dead stuck. Hoping I would wake up from this bad dream, I did not. It was all too real. I was near hyperventilation. Consuming my air far too quickly, passing out was a real possibility.

It is interesting what goes through your mind first in such "life and death" situations. I once almost had a patient bleed to death in my dental chair. Interestingly, I never actually touched this person. Any clinician worth their salt will confront such moments and need the composure to deal with them productively. Dead stuck in the restriction, my first thought was of the newspaper headline announcing my demise that boldly proclaimed, "Mounce died because he was stupid." What kind of jackass willingly goes into underwater caves, pays for it, gets dead stuck at 123 feet 1,100 feet back and then drowns? Imagine that legacy. Going out with such a whimper, my poor wife could have justifiably dug me up, put the whoop ass on me and then buried me again. A fate not unlike Oliver Cromwell, who, in 1860 after being dead for well over a year was dug up from Westminster Abbey in London, put in chains and subsequently beheaded! I would have deserved it.

Simultaneously, another terrifying awareness overcame me. I was blocking the exit for my dive guru! I had to clear the restriction so he could get out! This was our only exit. I could not be pulled through to the other side. I had no option but to get through and then back out.

Flailing about and panicking dead stuck 123 feet underwater is not productive. One problem under such stress can easily and quickly give birth to two others. Mr. Murphy (of Murphy's Law fame) lives in these caves and he is all too happy to kill a panicked diver. The warning sign at the entrance to many underwater caves has a picture of the Grim Reaper for a reason. The Grim Reaper warns divers to turn around unless they are trained and have the proper equipment. This is not an environment in which to hope that fortune will favor the foolish.

My second instinct after mentally penning my obituary was much more productive than the first. This second instinct was also called upon in the medical emergency above and gave birth to the steps I took to deal with it:

> 1) Control your breathing.
> 2) Assess the situation.
> 3) Assess your resources.
> 4) Make a plan.
> 5) Execute the plan.
> 6) Reevaluate the plan as needed.

This inner voice saved me. It was not entirely unlike Captain Kirk saying to Spock in the movie *Star Trek IV*, "Well, Spock, here we are, thanks to your restored memory and a little bit of good luck, we're walking the streets of San Francisco looking for a couple of humpback whales. How do you propose to solve this minor problem?" (Higham 73) How indeed did I propose to solve my minor problem of being dead stuck?

As a first step, I knew that I had to control my breathing. Mentally, I forced myself to breathe from my belly button and for the moment ignore that I was held in irons by the cave's rock walls. Even as my respiration slowed and I began to regain a modicum of composure, it was not at all intuitive as to how I was to free myself. Nevertheless, having slowed my breathing and taking smaller breaths, the decreased width of my chest made me smaller in diameter. I realized that I could make millimeter progress forward in concert with exhaling. This, combined with simultaneous physical gyrations probably resembling an unattractive fertility ritual, enabled me to gradually progress until I could see the other side of the restriction and my guru's dive light. After what took three minutes and yet seemed like three hours, I popped through. Only then could I contemplate what I had previously blocked out. I had to go back. With all the same terror that accompanied my entry, I was able to make my way back out of the restriction, clear the path and allow us both to emerge unharmed.

Chapter 3

Fear. The Spice of Life.

"Man is so made that whenever anything fires his soul, impossibilities vanish." (Weldon 126)

Jean De La Fontaine (1621 – 1695) (Pesonen)

When I was a kid, I remember my dad climbing the Douglas fir trees in our yard on Milton Street in Portland, Oregon, without safety ropes to hang his ham radio antennas. He was among the first Navy men in WWII to be part of UDTs, (underwater demolition teams) fusing, setting and defusing water mines. The UDTs were the forerunner of the Navy Seals. In his twenties, he was part of the allied invasion force of North Africa in 1942 and in the Pacific, starting in mid-1943. Dad saw action at Tarawa and the Battle of Okinawa. A private man, even when asked directly, he spoke very little about his experience of war. My dad had many qualities. Absolute fearlessness was one of them. He was not afraid to die. I like that.

Like my father, I decided many years ago that I could not directly control some things in this life, one of which is when I would die. I could try to maintain my fitness, physically and mentally, live in perfect harmony with God, man and nature, and yet still have my car flattened by a falling window-cleaning platform as actually happened at the Hancock building in Chicago in 2002. (Fountain) What a way to go, never see it coming and have absolutely no choice in the matter. How fair is that? It's not, but it is what is. I decided to live passionately without the fear of death. Being a believer, I accept that God will determine when it is time to take me from this earth. If the plane goes down, I am going to pray while it crashes and not flail about hysterically. If given a choice, I would prefer minutes of terror rather than months or years of treatment that will hurt those around me much more than me. I agree wholeheartedly with H. Rider Haggard who wrote "I am a fatalist, and believe that my time is appointed to come quite independently of my own movements, and that if I am to go to Suliman's Mountains to be killed, I shall go there and shall be killed there. God almighty, no doubt, knows His mind about me, so I need no trouble on that point." (Haggard 30) *While this passion to live fully without irrational fear is manifest as perseverance, it is a drive that has gotten me into trouble when not tempered by wisdom.*

In a clinical endodontic context, despite the best of intentions, some things go wrong. There is an old expression in our specialty, "You are only as good as your last case." What matters is to keep trying, learn from your mistakes and never fear an outcome that has not happened. In essence, you're not dead until you're dead, keep going.

Fear should spice our lives. It is not a stop sign.

I am puzzled by those who live controlled by unreasonable fear and walk within rigid boundaries of what they believe they can and cannot do. How can we know what we are capable of until we fail after doing our best? Using cave diving as a metaphor, how can a person let the underwater world or much of the world above water go unexplored out of fear or without at least wanting to know what is there? There is an important life lesson in this question for the extinguishing of all unnatural fear. Many fears are entirely baseless. The feared outcome never materializes or is of no consequence. How often do these unfounded fears paralyze us to the degree that they suck dry our human potential and make us lifeless shadows of what we could have been?

Trying to legislate all the danger and risk out of life robs us of something we desperately need as human beings, a spirit of adventure while moving toward something of wonder and value. Reaching a goal worth achieving means overcoming adversity, all of which builds a platform for evermore enriching experiences. I am convinced that there would be much less depression if we did not attempt to protect ourselves from every bump, bruise and struggle in life. We should accept that living entails risk, pain and stress. It simply does, despite our best efforts to either mask it or wish for the contrary. Literally, how many tons of legal and illegal substances and millions of gallons of alcohol are consumed every year to help people deal with situations that require intelligence and resolve? We grow only through adversity and effort. Hard knocks are essential for our development. We cannot know peace unless we know war. We cannot know victory unless we know defeat. We cannot know fullness unless we know need. We are never defeated until we are dead, and then our fate is in God's hands, not ours. Life asks us every day to step up to its plate to have a swing. How many of us answer that call to our full potential? Why do we recoil in fear? Why do we run from our trials or try to hide from the truth of our situations?

Fear implores me to slow down, consider the facts, evaluate the options, weigh the risks and then make a plan. Ultimately though, it encourages me to jump with a running start. If we prepare ourselves well, when action is truly called for, little should surprise us. To quote Ralph Waldo Emerson, "Do the thing you fear and the death of fear is soon to follow." (Hansen 82) It is the only way to grow. I refuse to stand on the sidelines and give in to fear. If God decides that it's time to take me home because I zigged when I should have zagged while cave diving, so be it, at least I died living passionately. That makes me uniquely me. It is one of the things that my loved ones appreciate about me. I refuse to let fear rule my activities and determine what I can and cannot achieve. If I let fear prevent me from cave diving, what above ground do I also give myself license to be afraid of and avoid? What is safe for me? Out of irrational fear I may miss something that keeps me from being fully human, from being what God intended. Where do I draw the line to say that I can or cannot do something? How do I know if I never try? We must test ourselves in life's battles to know what we are capable of. To acquire any skill, we must go through awkwardness and often pain to achieve proficiency. Being passive, when action is clearly called for drains our self-esteem. It is an opportunity lost. We cannot build a winning mentality if we turn tail and run.

This is not a *carte blanche* invitation to be stupid or to risk something that we cannot afford to lose, like our lives or intimate relationships. Rather, using my cave diving as an example, mastering irrational fear provides an opportunity for enrichment. Much of my dive training has been uncomfortable, awkward and yet absolutely necessary. I cannot gain the pleasure of diving that I have related elsewhere in *Dead Stuck* and yet not pay the price needed to earn the right to be there. During dive training, I have thrown up many times from nausea. My air supply has been turned off both accidently and in training drills. I have been tangled in lines and wrecks to the extent of being temporarily immobilized. I have spent my share of time blinded underwater using only tactile feel to navigate my way simulating zero visibility. I was scared shitless going down my first highly inclined cave passage, not to mention being dead stuck. But like all failures and challenges, these have provided me with enough knowledge and skill to know that I can handle all that is within my level of certification and that I have no right, to quote the famous dentist G.V. Black, "to be other than a continuous student." (Black 875)

In a poorly thought out decision, I chose to major in Chemistry at Santa Clara University. While Santa Clara is an outstanding school, and I have fond memories of my time there, chemistry did not broaden my understanding of culture, humanity, literature or the world beyond me. Studying chemistry did not make me a more compassionate human being. Other than organic chemistry, it was drudgery. A solid anchorman, I worked twice as hard as the brainiacs surrounding me for often a lesser grade. But a science degree (or at least the minimum science requirement) was necessary to get into dental school.

Much of my dental school experience was a marathon of pushing wet spaghetti uphill. Dissecting cadavers that reeked of formaldehyde on Monday mornings in gross anatomy as a freshman dental student or watching autopsies in the basement of the VA hospital in downtown Chicago did not float my boat. I did it because I had to.

Many dental school classes were the perfect tonic to insomnia. In my era, lectures were often given in dark rooms containing 120 exhausted, heavy breathing dental students. Some slides were in black and white. Especially after lunch, when the room would warm up in what was often the fourth lecture of the same day, it was "Boom Boom (Out Go The Lights)" (Boom Boom by Pat Travers). I did not stay awake for a single entire lecture after my freshman year. Sleep deprivation was a staple of dental school life at that time. I doubt much has changed now. Being as fair as possible to some of my teachers, staying awake was not such a great bargain either. To remain conscious meant hearing dismally boring lectures on removable partial denture design and the chemistry of impression materials, thankfully dental subjects as far removed from my work today as an endodontist as humanly possible.

Being a general dentist, however, led me to endodontics, a place where I truly belong. I would have never gotten here if I had let my fear, anxiety or distaste of the moment get the better of me. When it mattered, I had to both perform and persevere, even when I viscerally disliked it.

My personal failures in marital relationships were a painful prerequisite to getting it right with my wife, Laura, a journey described in part in later chapters. We would not be together without the lessons learned from my previous mistakes.

I would never trade my perseverance for more of any popular measuring stick of success. With all due respect to Brad, Angelina, Tom, George and Leonardo, I do not want to be them. I want to be me. I believe in myself. I have proven myself, to myself, over and over. I can rely on myself when the chips are down. That makes me a good servant to others, starting with my wife and children and extending into the world. But to get to this place of value and service I have had to push through fear, challenge and discomfort (exactly like Brad, Angelina Tom, George and Leonardo). Like them, I could not have one without the other.

It is in the forward momentum of trying even when it hurts in the pursuit of a righteous goal that we emerge smarter, stronger and more capable. Avoiding the physical and mental stress that stands between our desired goal and us is far more damaging than pushing through it. No matter what, we are going to have pain and stress in this life. Rather than view this truth with disdain or fear, we can, if we submit, harness these to be our cornerstones in the pursuit of something worth having. The trick is to choose the right adversity to push through and use it for a purpose that benefits others. Lack of initiative brings the slow decay of stagnation. Pushing oneself away from fear and toward pleasure is a powerful motivator to fulfillment. Does not the possibility of genuine affection, desire, connection and warmth wait on the other side of a breakup we know should happen but which we are avoiding? Cannot the good things we seek pull us through the fear and obstacles to reach them?

A cynical reader might retort: "This guy is off his rocker. He just doesn't understand my situation! He does not know me; he does not know how much pain I am in right now. He doesn't know what I've been through and what's been done to me. He doesn't know how badly I've been abused. His ideas won't work for me." If this is true, what are you doing to change? How do you expect your reality to change if you do not change your thinking and behavior? Other than the past, what present strategies do you have moving forward? Are you being truthful with yourself about your present situation? Are you where you really want to be? No worries if you do not like my ideas. But if not mine, then whose, and when? What are you waiting for?

Chapter 4

Football Addiction and the Miracle at Highbury

"The most incredible thing about miracles is that they happen." (Chesterton)

G.K. Chesterton (1874 – 1936) (Ribstein)

My love of world football has been a strong asset when I lecture globally in endodontics. Male dentists outside North America tend to be football fans. They look at me quizzically when I know of their nation's famous players and teams. It develops instant rapport. Dropping Dimitar Berbatov's[5] name in Sofia, Bulgaria, makes an audience sit up and listen in a way that looking down at them from the American ivory tower never could. Knowing that Chivas of Guadalajara, Mexico, has a local rival team, Atlas, and describing when I saw Atlas play at the Jalisco stadium lets a local audience there know that I may have some small glimmer into their everyday life.

Football is played with a round ball on a "pitch"[6] not on a "field." I am a red blooded American, and I consider myself a patriot. In real football though, known stateside as "soccer," my blood is English and the bulldog spirit lives within.

I have never been to an NFL game, nor have I seen more than two minutes of any Super Bowl much less been to a Super Bowl party or contributed to a betting pool. In any given year, I could not tell you who is in the game, much less how they got there. I have seen two college Division I NCAA football games live. One of those was a blowout. In October 1981, I witnessed my dental alma mater, Northwestern, lose to Iowa 64-0 in Evanston, Illinois, on a sunny but cold Saturday afternoon. (Sorensen) Obviously, in those days the Wildcats were better at training dentists than football players. I would be hard pressed to name more than half of the NFL, NBA, NHL and MLB franchises. March Madness, the national college basketball tournament, passes without my knowing who was mad at whom. I know who Tiger is and that Lance won seven tours. I know that cars are integral to Formula 1, but I do not watch ESPN nor listen to sports talk radio. I am an American beer company's nightmare; they have no hope of reaching me through domestic sports advertising.

In the 2001 Metro-Goldwyn-Mayer comedy *Bandits*, Billy Bob Thornton wakes up from a dream saying, "Beavers and Ducks" in reference to the University of Oregon Ducks and Oregon State University Beavers (Bandits 2001). These public state universities are fierce archrivals. Perhaps synchronicity was at play when an alcoholically lubricated woman and her friend once approached me in a bar earnestly asking "Ducks or Beavers?" This was an original pickup line if ever I have heard one, a line spiced with both substance and style. Quite clearly, this did not happen while I was living in my "Man Wears Girl Repellant" era detailed elsewhere. "Beavers," I replied. Speaking to her friend, "For you, Ducks." I was right. I knew. How I knew is a different story, but in the state of Oregon, "Ducks or Beavers?" is a provocative question of social significance. It says a great deal about you, not unlike if you are a Yankees or Red Sox fan. Supporting both of these teams is a wholly incompatible, "chalk and cheese" proposition. The University of Oregon and Oregon State University play a sold out "Civil War" football game each fall. With all due respect to both teams, I would much rather spend the afternoon watching polo, synchronized swimming or Olympic curling than sit in the rain seeing these boys crunch each other on the gridiron. I am not sure what a gridiron is, but I know it does not make waffles and I do not want to hit even one at high speed.

When I listen to "jock talk" at corporate dinners, I might as well be hearing Chinese. I often have no clue about the athletes or events discussed. On these occasions I am listening and physically present, but mentally my head is in the Santiago Bernabéu in Madrid, Old Trafford in Manchester, the San Siro in Milan, Wembley in London and the Maracanã in Rio De Janiero, just a few of the majestic cathedrals in which I have seen live competitive football matches. These matches are what we football purists call *joga bonito* in Portuguese, "the beautiful game." Football is the world's game. It is my game, my passion and my second religion.[7] Turn the subject to "footie" as it is known in Britain, and I light up like the space shuttle at liftoff. The Red Devils of Manchester United (from Manchester, England)[8], affectionately known as "Man Yoo," are my team. They play in the English Premier League, the richest and arguably most competitive league in the world. For those who are not sure, God lives in the red half of Manchester and he speaks to Sir Alex Ferguson, their manager, on a regular basis. [9-10-11]

My romance with football had its origins many years ago when I was in college. Before the Internet, laptop computers, cell phones, Twitter, text messaging and the technology that we now take for granted, I had a small black and white 12" television with a hangar for an antenna. Every Saturday at 4 p.m., an English football match was shown that had been condensed into 60 minutes from the usual game time of 90. For an hour, I was transported to another world in my dorm room, a place I would later come to appreciate as "Planet Football."

Like meeting a woman and slowly over time coming to appreciate her qualities, I grew to appreciate the subtle textures of football's character. Initial appearances can deceive. I found the game to be anything but boring. Football grew to resonate deeply within me. As the week progressed, I found my private thoughts slipping back to relive some moment I had recently seen in a match, a moment I would often replay for its triumph or tragedy. I came to understand what happens on the pitch mirrors life off of it. The comparisons are striking. For example, life is not fair. Some refereeing decisions during matches are not fair. A person can perform extremely well at a task within a working group and the project still fail. A football team can collectively perform well and yet lose the match through one mistake or bad luck. Creativity, effort and innovation can certainly change any given day in one's life for the better. A moment of brilliance on the pitch can turn a match on its head. While I am sure others see these parallels in American sports, the association between the two domestically has never been clear to me.

In world football the aim is never to hit or injure the opposition. The violence inherent in American football is not present in world football although there is just, if not much more passion and intensity in the spectacle.[12] While this is not to say that severe injuries do not occur, the game is only designed to put the ball in the back of the net. A line of civility is drawn in the sand in world football that is rarely breached even in the most contentious international matches. While not a criticism of American football, this is an attribute that has spoken to me since the days of my 12" black and white television.

Over time, I also came to realize that scoring a goal while never using a hand requires immense skill and fitness to perform at the highest level. Bringing a 40-yard pass down from mid air with one touch and striking the ball toward the goal and scoring with a second is breathtaking to watch. While there are many such moves and skills that take place continuously throughout a game, having played a fair bit of recreational soccer I appreciate how refined and practiced these skills are. At the highest level, they are a sporting equivalent to the sublime mastery displayed in other non-sporting art forms.

My initial infatuation with the game slowly grew to obsession. I won't sugar coat it, I am addicted to football and primarily to the Man Yoo strain of the virus. I have toured Old Trafford twice and seen numerous games there live. Even though I respect them, I could meet President Barack Obama, Bono or Bill Gates, all at once or separately, and never break a sweat. By contrast, I would probably wet myself if I met the players in the Man Yoo locker room. For a gainfully employed married father of two living on the west coast of North America, without mental illness or a criminal record, possessing respectable credit, to idolize Roy Keane, Eric Cantona, Cristiano Ronaldo and Patrice Evra, to name a few of the United players past and present, is just plain daft.[13]

My will directs my ashes be spread at the Stretford end of Old Trafford.[14] I am sure this is against the law and will subject my heirs to arrest, but that is a minor detail in the grand scheme of things. I suggested to my children, Alana and Bianca, when they were younger that they take the Old Trafford tour over and over, put a small hole in their pockets and let little bits of me scatter around the ground, stands and especially the locker room. This nutty idea was rapidly kyboshed[15] by the girls. They are a bit smarter than their father. I conveniently choose to ignore the fact that my ashes will be swept up into the dustbin. Nevertheless, until I get a better plan, this is my strategy going forward.

I follow the teams every move. I know not only the game schedule but also when the team is actually on the field playing. If the game is televised and I am home, irrespective of the time of day or what else needs doing, I create a bubble to watch. Everything else stops. England is usually eight hours ahead of the West Coast of North America. Some games are shown live with a 12 noon or more commonly a 3 p.m. kick off. Doing the math reveals that more than once I have been up early glued to the big screen. Praise God most of the games are on Saturday and that not every one is televised live. If the match has already been played and I have not seen it, I have idiosyncratic rules for playing the tape. I only watch if they win or come from behind to get a draw. I will not watch the game on tape if I do not know the outcome. When they lose, I will not see the highlights, nor will I read the report; it is simply too painful. What would I accomplish in doing so? I cannot change the result. As if I were on the team, in my head and heart, I kick every ball. I go up for every header. I try to stop every shot. I slide in for every tackle. I talk to the players during the match telling them who on the opposing team is unmarked.[16] As if I were the manager, I select transfer targets and decide whom I would like to buy and sell. Mentally, I draw up the roster for any given match day. I check the table[17] frequently. I know not only where we are in the standings, but also by how many points, any games in hand and our goal difference. I could name the entire Man Yoo first team likely to start on any given Saturday, who should be on the substitute's bench, who is injured and when they should return. I could probably tell you whether the player was bought from another team and roughly for how much, their nationality or whether they were a product of the club's youth academy.

My wife, Laura, is given daily reports on issues surrounding the club. For example, I tell her about such timely subjects as the status of Wayne Rooney's hamstring problem, whether the Brazilian playmaker Anderson (Anderson Luís de Abreu Oliveira) will need surgery, or whether the svelte Bulgarian Dimitar Berbatov was a good buy at £30.75 million. (Man Utd complete Berbatov switch) When Man Yoo win, the sun shines more brightly, my step has more spring and my week goes better. It is almost as if the earth spins on its axis with more stability.

Once on a tour of England, I went to their previous training ground, the Cliff, to watch them practice before they moved into their new facilities at Carrington. I stood with a number of children to get autographs from the players. When they came to America for their summer tour in 2003, I attended their open practice and did the same. I could have shaken hands with Sir Alex as he stood two feet from me, but I was afraid I might babble like an idiot before a Knight. During this same tour, I arranged a road trip and took a van full of friends to Seattle to see them demolish Glasgow Celtic 4-0. (Man Utd thump Celtic)

I religiously tape Sky Sports on television for the latest from the world of English football. My Internet home page is the BBC football site. I check the Man Yoo stories first, followed immediately by the daily football gossip link. On any given day I revel in the daily tales of players being "tapped up,"[18] rumors of club takeovers, managerial comings and goings, arrests for assault and corruption, details about who is trying to buy and sell players and who has slagged off [19] whom in the last 24 hours.[20-21]

English cabbies look at me incredulously when I chat their national game with the fluency of a native. Their reaction is not unlike that of a local hearing an American speaking flawless Nepalese on the streets of Kathmandu.[22] All of this said, with one notable personal exception, because I am not English, I have never been nor will I ever be accepted into the true clique of British football fans, just as any foreigner who may have lived in a country for many years is never truly a local. In light of this story though, I am a strong candidate for an honorary knighthood for football support above and beyond the call of duty. [23]

The Miracle at Highbury

While truth is indeed stranger than fiction, I admit I once promised Jesus that I would reform my life if Man Yoo could score against Arsenal at Highbury.[24] The day was February 1, 2005. I had arranged an endodontic lecture tour to have me in London for the match live. Any true Man Yoo fan hates three teams: Liverpool, Manchester City and the Gunners of Arsenal. As games go, this was a big one, with both teams challenging for the title. The match was lit for a powder keg.

A massive and permanent banner at Old Trafford reads "MUFC, the Religion." Standing in the Man Yoo section at Highbury for at the match, I was surrounded by several thousand like-minded faithful. I respect the Arsenal manager, Arsene Wenger, but it is rather peculiar that even when his players commit grievous acts of barbarity in full view of even the most distant spectator, he never sees it even though he has the best view in the house. He also never seems to have seen the replay of his players committing these acts. For Arsene though, every offense committed against his team has been microscopically examined and its travesty expressed in the most somber terms in the post match interview. He also has an annoying habit of saying he will support his players even when they perpetrate the aforementioned thuggery. Recently though, he has admitted to "selective vision." "At times I saw it, and I said I didn't to protect the player...It's because I could not find any rational explanation to defend him." (Wenger admits to 'selective vision') His admission confirms what we Man Yoo fans have known all along. He saw everything.

Unknown to the crowd at the time, before the kickoff, there had been an incident in the tunnel leading out onto the pitch as the teams came out from the dressing rooms. Roy Keane[25] had squared up to Patrick Viera[26] to protect Gary Neville.[27] Neville is much shorter than Viera. Apparently, Viera had been verbally abusing Neville. This event, available on YouTube, is known as the "tunnel incident." These titans were separated to avoid it escalating into a boxing match. Keane and Viera, in their day, were arguably two of the best midfield players in the world. Keane retired in 2006. (Reaction to Keane's retirement) At this writing, Viera was still playing in Italy. Ali and

Frazier-like is not an entirely exaggerated statement of their rivalry and competitiveness. It warms my heart, as it does all Man Yoo supporters, to see a smaller Roy Keane in the video wagging his finger at Patrick Viera and being kept apart by the referee Graham Poll. Man Yoo scored first and Arsenal went on to notch two unanswered goals and led United 2-1 into the 50th minute. With the second Arsenal goal, my spirit sank. It was unconscionable that we could lose with my having traveled half way around the world to see this very game. I was just not down for this! Man Yoo are my boyz, my crew; they could not lose, not here, not now and not to the Gunners of Arsenal. I had to do something. But what could I do? We needed a miracle, and we needed it posthaste. As the situation grew more desperate, looking into the London night sky, I had an inspiration. I knew what to do. I could help my team. I decided to pray and ask for divine intercession. Closing my eyes, I said to Jesus, "I'll make you a deal, if you let us draw or get a win here tonight, I will reform my life and go where you lead me. Pinky double swear." At church, I have heard the expression, "You've got to conceive it to receive it." How I conceived it, I do not know. That I would even consider asking Jesus to cut such a bargain is beyond my comprehension. Nevertheless, He answered me, and a miracle occurred.

The Red Devils of Man Yoo scored three unanswered goals in the second half, the first almost immediately after I lifted up my prayer. As the game went on, with every Man Yoo goal, complete strangers embraced. Beer, bad breath and body odor were liberally dispersed among the joyful masses. We sang with the abandon of drunken pirates. I was speechless; I could not believe what I was seeing. If Jesus himself had been playing for United that evening, such a confluence of luck, guts, skill and grit would have been hard to improve upon. My team showed the world that they possessed bags of self-belief in their abilities to claw their way back into the match. Not only had they won, but also they did so with one of their players, Mikel Silvestre, sent off for fouling an Arsenal player who coincidently rolled around like a boneless chicken from the merest of contact. Man Yoo went on to win the title for the 2004-2005 season.

It is a cliché that fact is stranger than fiction. This is fact; it actually happened. What is doubly ironic is that I did return to church and work actively to deepen my faith, an effort that I continue daily. I have asked myself many times, was this just coincidence? Did this comeback have a deeper meaning? Was it a sign from God that if I had faith the size of a mustard seed that amazing things could happen? Some might say that the statistical odds of a comeback, while grossly unfavorable, played out that evening, that the cosmic and karmic one-armed bandit of life hit my number. Others might put it down to the rational explanation, that on the evening, Arsenal had no answers for the questions asked by Man Yoo. The better team won; there was nothing else at play. Some might argue coincidence. It just happened.

Unshaken and unquestioning faith and belief in miracles do not come easily to me. Being an endodontist, I am a professional skeptic. I have to be. I have been trained to see the flaws in previous root canal treatment, to find incongruities between what patients tell me and their objective examination findings. Lacking skepticism is a formula for clinical disaster. Being almost 50 at the time of this writing, my life experience has made me question almost everything I see, read, feel and experience to measure its veracity. I am not given to cheap belief in anything. After two divorces and two broken engagements, suffice it to say, developing the trust needed to marry was an endeavor with risk and needed time. Laura, my wife, God bless her, was up to the task. While I would like to think that I am open minded, having been deceived and disappointed as we all have been, I admit I would be like the Apostle Thomas needing to put his finger in Jesus' wounds to prove that he had risen.

Did Jesus turn water into wine at Cana? Did the Red Sea part before Moses? Did the Virgin Mary appear to a young girl at Fatima in Portugal? Did the Son of God come down to allow our sins to be forgiven by being hung on a cross? If so, why did God show himself to us in this way? Why not just write a book with the story of evolution that would eliminate all doubt about where we came from? More importantly, why? How did Man Yoo score three goals in a match that seemed to be slipping out of their hands and in which they were behind until my prayer was lifted? These are all good questions, ones that require blind faith. These are queries for which I have no answers.

My doubting nature aside, what I saw cannot be explained rationally. I do not believe it occurred by chance. It was not a freak accident of statistical probability. I am willing not to question it. I am willing to allow what happened to just be, to not attempt to tear apart the otherwise imponderable. If it was not a miracle, it was as close to a miracle as I have ever seen. Something transcendent happened on that evening, which is clearly what God is, the alpha and the omega, something beyond my understanding. At the end of the day, this miracle is one reason, among many, that make me say, "I believe."

Besides, after coming on as a substitute, John O'Shea, a versatile defensive utility player, exquisitely chipped the ball over Arsenal goalkeeper Manuel Almunia in the 89th minute of the match to score Man Yoo's fourth goal and seal a 4-2 win. Even more improbably, he looked the most gifted striker on the planet in doing so. Now that is a miracle indeed. He probably still cannot believe it either. God answers prayer. Amen.

Chapter 5

Man Wears Girl Repellent

"Drinking makes such fools of people, and people are such fools to begin with, that it's compounding a felony." (Prochnow 129)

Robert Benchley (1889 – 1945) (Yates 165)

When we are young, we do not believe we will get older. It happens to others, just not to us. Young, invincible and full of swagger, when aging crosses our minds, we immediately block it out, its prospect too chilling for contemplation. I was no different. Throw disposable income onto my hubris, along with my being an unmarried endodontist at the time, and a recipe for misadventure was born.

This story happened many years ago. Men think things that they would never tell anyone, not their best male friends and certainly not their wives or girlfriends. This story lifts the curtain on some of those thoughts. This reveals where I was at that time in my life. Reading it still makes me belly laugh. Youth is wasted on the young. (qtd. in Keyes 257) *I was younger then.*

What follows is true, all of it. Pinky swear, it happened just this way.

The absolute nadir of my single life occurred when I was about to begin making time with an attractive 29-year-old female ER physician. I had flown to New England to visit a close and platonic female friend who was attending a farewell party for one of her departing co-workers. Knowing only my friend, I walked into an off-the-shelf Home Depot kitchen filled with a diverse assortment of people who, like me, earned their living wearing scrubs. The medical brother and sisterhood collected on this fine evening were decidedly upbeat. Happily chatting, the group was guzzling goodly quantities of wine coolers, hard cider, kegged beer and tequila shots. These same tequila shots later became the knife-edge on which this sad tale later turns.

Having been single for years, I was open to meeting a woman in the

Armchair Adventures and Miracles

midst of the longest running relationship drought of my life. Living a stretch of bad form equivalent to a major league hitter going 0-30, if I were a *National Enquirer* headline, it would have shouted: "Man Wears Girl Repellent." Think Mojave Desert. Dry. How does one define "drought" or "slump" in the relationship context? Let me count the ways. At that stage in my life, if I were to walk into a club, women were parting like the Red Sea before Moses. Dance or make idle chat with me? No chance. The last 50 women of all flavors around the world I had asked to dance or tried to chat up had given me reasons why they were challenged in dancing and chatting that ranged from the ridiculous to the sublime. My rap was tragic. I thought that dance clubs and bars were ostensibly places for meeting people, but I must have missed something. Ironically, after my being given the ice treatment, I often observed the same women sashay up to the next cowboy at the bar. There is an old expression that "Even a blind squirrel finds an acorn sometimes" (Richard W. Thorington 149), a sentiment much like the gravitational fact that the sun shines on a dog's bum every once in a while if he is lucky. At this time, things were not going my way. Going into the evening, this dog's bum had seen no sun.

My grave predicament did have a lighter side though. The last two situations where sleeping with a woman or playing "high school screw" as my Dad once called it, (meaning any kind of nookie in his vernacular) was even a remote possibility prompted rejections that rated medal status in the Olympic category of "excuses." The Gold Medal recipient for excuse No. 1 was that the woman could not sleep with me because she could not protect her heart and would be crushed if we dated, had sex and then broke up, so strong was her desire to have a future romantic relationship. She also mentioned in the same breath that if I were any ordinary yokel on the street she would be off like a shot for the sack. Even though I was better than chocolate, she just could not. The Silver Medalist for excuses claimed that despite the fact that she had shagged anything with a penis for the past six years she needed to begin being a good girl somewhere. I was it, her new gauntlet of chastity. One other pair of encounters is worthy of an Honorable Mention. Two women, independently of one another, each told me, within a two week period, that they would, how do I put this delicately, enthusiastically engage in a certain oral act and swallow, but just not so soon or that night. I do not need to tell you how either of these encounters ended. My suspicion is that each of these women had read the same *Cosmopolitan* article detailing methods to keep a guy on the bubble

43

Dead Stuck

while they waited for their lost true love. In the "meeting women" derby, by a country mile, my horse was bringing up the rear.

Mingling politely, I settled into the evening and became intertwined in conversations ranging from heartbreaking to sidesplitting. Revelers detailed the loss of a treasured hunting dog hit by a car to how a man had been intubated while only suffering from low blood sugar. Rather than feeling the odd man out, I was quite enjoying the festivities. Being an outsider who would not come this way again gave me a swagger increasingly lubricated with each drink. Despite my chutzpah, the odds were seemingly not in my favor. Most of the women at the party were accompanied by the usual assortment of husbands, boyfriends, wannabes and himbos. This was not a "target rich environment" in the Tom Cruise *Top Gun* context. (Paramount Pictures, 1986) Meeting a woman did not appear on the cards. Being an optimist for whom hope springs eternal, I believed that things could only get better. But could they?

Despite the husbands and himbos, in addition to the attractive 29-year-old female ER physician, there was one contender, a single woman, clad with a midriff top sporting a belly ring. If I had not known better, she looked as though she was practicing for a dry humping competition. It was difficult not to stare at what resembled the sequel to *Dirty Dancing*. (Vestron Pictures, 1987) Her jeans were at least two sizes too tight. The whole thing looked painful. Our introduction immediately went up in smoke. Upon shaking, I instantly received the stink eye matched by her first words: "Oh, cold hand." Holding my beer with the same hand I used to shake proved my undoing. Perhaps she thought I was a mortician and wanted none of that. Shot down in flames, the severity of my slump was reaffirmed. My inner child was proving flawed, a defect manifested in my man meets woman wearing midriff dry humping etiquette.

A few minutes after the cold hand debacle, I was invited to take a tequila shot with several people. People whom, curiously enough, looked like they needed one. Included was the aforementioned attractive 29 year-old ER physician. Apparently, the conversation just before pouring the shot had drifted into the vein of how this woman should "lighten up, enjoy life and live a little." People always use such cheery repartee to engage others in nefarious endeavors like downing tequila. Apparently, the other tequila shooters felt that the key to discovering the meaning of this young doctor's life could be found alongside the worm at the bottom of a small children's juice cup brimming with tequila.

Pardon the short digression, but as a teenager I once drank almost four bottles of Cold Duck champagne in a three-hour period. How much exactly I drank and how long it took, at this point, are a bit fuzzy for obvious reasons. Suffice it to say I was well beyond a mere three sheets to the wind. While the names of the guilty that aided and abetted this madness will remain undisclosed, exactly like the tequila shots above, it seemed like a good idea at the time. For a few minutes, somewhere into the third bottle, I was Paul Rodgers (of Free, Bad Company and the Firm, not to mention the new and improved Queen plus Paul Rodgers fame) belting out "All Right Now" to a sleeping Portland from on top of Rocky Butte, one of the city's best venues to watch submarine races.[28] (Free, All Right Now, 1970) Vicariously, I was transported to the Isle of Wight Festival circa 1969 in front of over 100,000. (Isle of Wight Festival History 1969) We can, for the purposes of brevity, gloss over the fact that in 1969, while Paul was strutting for the masses, I was all of 10 years old. It was my "rock and roll fantasy." (Google Music: Bad Company, 10 from 6, 1985)

Many bad ideas, such as drinking almost four bottles of Cold Duck, get their genesis with meager forethought and total disregard to the consequences. I am eternally lucky and grateful that no harm came to me or anyone else. As a passenger driving home, I saw four lights at every traffic stop and was literally poured into bed. We might have gotten away with it except that my accomplices dropped my boots on the floor with a mighty thud and woke my parents. The crashing of my boots aside, my friends' uproarious laughter during my deposition into bed did little to disguise how plastered we were except for the designated driver.

Adding insult to injury, I had promised my sister I would play racquetball at 6 a.m. the next morning after being out on the piss.[29] Painfully and miraculously, I did play and managed to do so only seeing one ball. I was comprehensively shellacked. Green for the next two days, it would be literally decades before I could touch champagne again. To this day I can count on one hand my sips of bubbly since serenading a sleeping Portland wearing bell-bottoms to "All Right Now." (Free, All Right Now, 1970)

Not unlike my adventure on Rocky Butte, aiding and abetting were indeed both perpetrated in encouraging the attractive 29-year-old ER physician to imbibe. She took the prodding of the nursing staff to unwind seriously. Possessing short dark hair and intelligent but sorrowful eyes, this thoughtful woman of medium height was unfailingly polite and brimming with a persona that said, "Yes, I am a capable doctor, but something is missing." My intuition told me that she was a solid citizen, the person you wanted to handle your guts if they were splattered about on the sidewalk.

Dead Stuck

She could be trusted. Her clothes were sensible enough, black jeans and an orange turtleneck that spoke of a climb of Himalayan proportions. As the tequila eased into her bloodstream, she was visibly aroused in posture and demeanor. An epiphany seemed to be arising from within her. Watching her, my gut told me that she realized she was missing some of the good things in life. She was having fun, perhaps even for the first time in her life. She had been a good girl, followed the rules, dissected the frog in high school with reckless abandon and scored high on the MCATs.[30] All this to reach the highest pinnacle of her life thus far, doing tequila shots in this suburban New England kitchen. But what else was the girl to do? Go home and read her textbooks? I think not! If the journey of a lifetime starts with a single step, she was ready to sprint.

Sensing her emerging moment of clarity, I decided to take a chance and ask her (not even knowing her name and having shared nothing with her except a healthy shot of Mexican firewater) if she was happy and what she wanted out of life. Looking at me incredulously but most sincerely, she replied she was happy and did know what she wanted out of life. In the next nanosecond she blurted out the truth, "No and I don't have a clue!" "Ah, hah!" I thought, now we were getting somewhere. Her answer made me take a much more fatal stab in the dark. A stab that I knew might either get me slapped or, if I was lucky, make a friend. Trying to be suave, I asked, "Let me see if I understand. You have been good all your life. You have done everything asked of you. You are a full-fledged doctor with responsibility over life and death. You carry the weight of the world on your shoulders. But you are not having much fun. You're asking yourself if this is all there is, just a job and a paycheck. You do not have the passion and joy you expected from your career. You want an exciting life, but you are not sure how to get started. Am I close?" Expecting a cuff across the face or a look of amazement at my keen clairvoyance, imagine my joy when she wobbled on her feet, unable to meet my searching gaze. She quickly regained her composure. When she could look me in the eye, she replied, "Yes, exactly, and how do you know that about me? Nobody has ever figured that out before!"

While women have their sporting metaphors, there are moments in a man's life when he knows that he has performed the equivalent of hitting a grand slam to win the World Series by a single run in game seven in the bottom of the 9th with a full count and two outs for the Yankees against the Red Sox. Being a world football (soccer) fan, I had just nailed a bicycle kick from the penalty spot to score the winning golden goal (sudden death)

46

for England in the World Cup final to beat Germany at the end of the second overtime in Munich at the Olympic stadium. Made them Germans eat raw sauerkraut! Such a feat is *muy macho*, mondo studly. It would be a moment unrivaled in world football history. At that moment, I was Pele, Georgie Best, Zizou, Puskas, Distefano[31] and Gary Lineker among a host of other soccer luminaries all rolled into one. In my soul, I had just slid on the wet grass on my knees after scoring with my fists clenched to the thunderous roar of the traveling England fans. My knighthood was secured. One of the stands at Wembley[32] was already being renamed for me, my number retired.

Given the depth of my recent dreadful slump, imagine the elation and adrenaline rush that followed knowing that I had just slotted home the aforementioned screamer from a half chance.[33] I had confirmed a true brilliance that the last 50 women I had tried to chat with just simply could not see. My Walter Mitty[34] football fantasy aside, my pride exploded. I had done something of real merit. I was a man among men. My head, heart and gut not only said, "Yeah baby!" in unison, but "Come to papa!" "Cowabunga!" "Holy cow!" and a wide range of other such stupid male affirmations of success. I wanted to punch the sky, as footballers often do when they score a goal. I had connected with this attractive 29-year-old ER physician.

My self-control got the better of me. Punching the air in the kitchen at that moment was a really bad idea and I knew it. But her positive response to my overture was a moment to savor. I still had mojo baby! I still had it down where men really live. My sperm was delta force commando bold roasted, not the decaffeinated post-vasectomy variety. This half-Italian blue-eyed boy with a bit too much gut still had a little woman wooing ability. My toes tingled. I felt like a rock band in the mold of Def Leppard being able to tour again and have somebody actually pay to hear my songs 20 years after they were legitimate hits. The 401K-reunion tour could wait; I was still playing the big stadiums.

It is fair for the reader to ask at this point what my true intentions were. As a father of two daughters, if I were her father, I would want to know. Rest assured, I would never have told her what to do with her life. Women need to make their own choices. They do not need to be told what to do and it helps to know that they are always right. To argue with them, to tell them what to think or do, is to risk hell's most lethal fury. Simply put, no man at any time in history ever won an argument with a woman or ever changed a woman's mind. I was not going to be so presumptuous as to change the course of human history in this New England kitchen. I would not tell her what to do with her life or how to squeeze the juice out of the mundane routine of the ordinary everyday. I said what I did because I understood her, my professional school life and residency being much like hers. I also had been the dutiful child. I did what I was told, never questioning authority. Like Diego Maradona[35] who wanted to leave the shantytown of Villa Fiorito on the outskirts of Buenos Aires, I wanted to leave the circumstances of my upbringing. (James Dart) Part of what made my incisive armor-piercing strike down the heat shaft of her consciousness was that my experience mirrored hers. I knew a conforming child when I saw one. All the above said, men decide in seconds whether they would and could have sex with a woman and vice versa. Yes, I would have considered sleeping with her in due time. But a loose cruiser I am not. Despite my dating slump, I craved soulful connection. Anything else, a kiss included, was a bonus.

I learned the hard way early on that thinking with your anatomy is a dangerous pastime. This leads again to a short but essential tangent about trying to seduce women, drunken or otherwise, a sport as old as dirt. I once attended a men's retreat weekend (the details of which will remain private as we were sworn to secrecy) in which I stood buck nekkid in front of 35 men holding a phallic wooden penis. I began my story with "My dick's got me into a lot of trouble!" Once these words left my mouth, I was greeted with an enthusiastic roar of understanding and acceptance from the 35 other naked men in the room. A shared experience, almost everyone else's dick in that room had also gotten them into trouble. Viva la penis! United in our naked masculinity, it was quite a sight to behold! With the aforementioned troubled dick still attached to me, and wanting to keep it that way, I did not intend to menace this most pleasant young woman to peril of any sort.

I felt compelled to tell her my story. With faith, courage and work, I had found happiness. She could too. I wanted to tell her that we are not tied to the mast of our childhood traumas and that the best parts of life are at the pool's deep end. But to blurt out such heady paradigms at that very moment would have seemed rushed, like seeds planted at the wrong time and also thrown onto the rocks for good measure. I did not want to go from "Hello" to "Dr. Knows-it-All" in five minutes.

So as not to appear overeager, I walked away for a few minutes while the moment sank in, coincident with someone entering the conversation. If she was swooning from my remarkable insight and charms, I believed she would follow me. Later, I was to discover that leaving her at this juncture was my undoing. It seemed though, as do most plans that go astray, the correct strategy at the time.

Gone for a few minutes, I began a conversation with a young airline pilot about my hometown of Portland, Oregon, all the while trying to weave my way back into the fabric of her conversation on the other side of the room. It did not take long. After sorting out with the pilot that Portland did indeed 1) get a lot of rain, 2) was a nice place to raise kids and 3) was relatively clean and environmentally conscious with just the right amount of political correctness, I bid adieu to this "Does a bear shit in the woods?" conversation. Small talk is not my forte. We know the Pope is Catholic, why spend our time talking about it?

I meandered back to her neck of the woods, surprised that she had not followed me. My test had failed. Perhaps I had misinterpreted her? After a few minutes I was reassured when she turned to talk with me alone in front of the kitchen sink. Seemingly cold sober and yet alluringly interested in my every word and vice versa, she stood entirely too close for casual conversation. As our arms became intertwined, I stroked her back. A happy kitten, she purred.

Alcoholic fortification in the form of one glass of oak laden cabernet, three frosty bottles of Samuel Adams and one generous tequila shot encouraged me to open up to her further and see where this would lead. In Herman Melville's *Moby Dick*, it is said that it's "better sleep with a sober cannibal than a drunken Christian." (Melville 61) Despite my being one, on any given day, I would have to agree with him. Sober cannibal or drunken Christian aside, I knew that I could not share my whole life story with her in one breath. My head swirled. There was so much that I wanted to say and discover about her. I wanted to tell her that failure had made me much more humble and with a whole lot of failure under my belt I had desperately needed to find solutions to what were previously my unsolvable problems. Speaking the truth from one's heart has a way of evoking honest responses in return. I was so very ready to open up to her and speak from mine. I owned a catalogue of "Shooting Star" (Bad Company, Straight Shooter, 1975, "Shooting Star") rock-n-roll success, followed by downfall and then a subsequent redemption that coincided with a new and improved lifestyle. Quintessentially, I had undergone a rebirth of sorts, not unlike those seen on VH1 specials profiling fallen rock stars trying to make it a second time. My own dossier of personal self-destruction was impressive. It included two divorces, one near bankruptcy, an entire family not on speaking terms and two broken engagements. My healing and subsequent rise like a Phoenix from the ashes of these problems blended with what I perceived to be our similar childhoods allowed me to instantly and honestly engage this attractive 29-year-old ER physician.

So there we were, necking in a blissful state of mutual infatuation that, now outside its gravitational pull, can only be described as "cute." The nurses looking on were giggling, pointing at us from a distance, eyes smiling, and witnesses to something beautiful being born. For a man hungry to be touched, this was manna from heaven. The Buddhist in me has perfected the art of having no expectations and letting go of the outcome of any endeavor so as not to give it power over me. Having found an attractive woman wanting to crack open the shell of her life and possibly blossom with me was just too delicious. Expecting nothing, having had nothing, made finding something all the more pleasurable. I live and I suspect we all live in some measure for moments of soulful connection, unscripted and real, stripped naked of everything but raw truth. A kiss, in full public view, was imminent.

The white-hot flame of infatuation has a corresponding long-term reality (dishes, post partum depression, bad breath, soggy diapers, snoring, menopause, erectile dysfunction). The symbol of the Tao has two sides for a reason. I have never snorted cocaine nor done much of anything beyond smoking the obligatory hash as a tourist in Amsterdam. The hash notwithstanding, I am told that there is an equal and opposite crash to all highs. A crash that of course no one ever discusses when he or she is encouraging you to put yourself at risk of later having your nose rebuilt or some less appealing fate. The blissful, playful and transcendent warm fuzzy part of the story is over. Now comes the fall.

At the critical moment, two seconds before the luxuriant, silky wet kiss that surely must come, the 29-year-old ER physician took her lips away from my neck and to my left ear. Instead of whispering sweet nothings, telling me to take her upstairs or putting her lips against mine, she said, "I need to go throw up." The words struck me like a swift kick to the *cojones* on a sub-zero, wind chilled grey Siberian day with steel-toed boots.

While I was making witty and astute observations with the pilot about Portland, my newfound flame had been doing more tequila shots with the nurses in the guise of letting her hair down. She would later end up virtually comatose. With her immediate exit from the kitchen, she walked out of my life, forever. Such was my fate on this cold New England evening. Shortly after her departure, I left the party.

Hurling stories could fill up a novel or two on their own, but having worshipped the porcelain God a few times as a kid, I was completely sympathetic to the plight of her gastric mucosa. I was surprised, disappointed and reeling in disbelief. I was, up to that point, feeling that Allah, Buddha and Vishnu, not to mention the Holy Trinity and all the saints in heaven for that matter, had smiled on me. I was mistaken. Desperately unlucky or not, it just wasn't meant to be.

In the days that followed, my thoughts drifted back to how her breath felt on my neck, how close we were to kissing and how full of promise the moment was. A promise that proved empty. Trying to come to grips with what happened, I could only find solace in a football metaphor. In British football terms, there is the "fight back," a team that starts out poorly in a match and falls behind, seemingly so far that there is no hope of a recovery. This is manifest as being 3-1 or 3-0 down at half time and storming back to 3-3 with five minutes left. There is one minor problem, as often as not, the other team sucker punches you for a cheap counter-attacking goal while you surge forward for the winner and your team goes home 4-3 losers. In English football terms, as a Manchester United supporter, Liverpool had just won the league on the last day of the season on goal difference after we were 12 points ahead at Christmas. Ouch! I had been red carded by the Gods of love, sent off to an early shower for two questionable yellow cards.[36] Sometimes you play a good game and still get spanked like a puppy in training that piddled in the wrong place.

Puzzled and somewhat disoriented as time passed, I was not entirely sure what to do. I waited to see if she would contact me. With each passing day that she did not, I gradually lost hope. Now I doubt myself. Did I imagine it all? Did I remember something wrong? Did she feel anything? Did I represent something she was afraid of? Was she embarrassed? Did I misinterpret her? I will never know.

My rational brain tells me that if she felt anything she would have opened up to me while sober. Having made more than my share of idiotic and heroic gestures toward women over the years that failed, I decided that this is a sleeping dog I would let lie. There is an old Nepali proverb that states that when you find a piece of dried shit in the road, don't turn it over. Good coaching. I didn't take the advice; my attempts to contact her went unanswered. She never tried to contact me.

So, my story comes full circle and I end where I began. There is still no sun on this dog's bum. As I began my week at home, I had coffee in two days time with a recently divorced and badly wounded woman set up for me on a blind coffee date by one of my professional advisers. After five minutes on the phone I know that this will be a polite but sterile meeting. It is not my job to make this woman's heart open up again and accept love from me or anybody else. She is bitter and protective. She's been hurt. Some birds and angels with broken wings are better left alone until they heal. Perhaps this is unfeeling, perhaps arrogant, but I could honestly ask if I should be road kill in the healing of her heart and the restoration of her confidence?

My weekend doesn't look much better as I am scheduled to have dinner with a mysterious woman from the Midwest I met in a darkened hotel ballroom during a lecture. After being chatty Kathy, she rather brusquely refused to have lunch. Now comes the mystery. She has written me faithfully every Sunday for the past 18 months while never calling, not even once. She is traveling to my region of the country for a class. After initially acting like getting together for dinner was unimportant, she writes at the last minute to say she would like to make it happen with not so subtle tinges of flirtation. She has spurned my efforts over 18 months to propel this into anything more by coming up with the omnipresent trump card for these situations: the other man.

Guys know this Dosey Doe well, the boyfriend who emerges near the end of a dinner or coffee where the woman has decided she wants to keep you interested in her, but she is not sure for what or when. These boyfriends are usually described as a person with whom the woman has a deep emotional connection despite the relationship always being troubled and containing some lingering uncertainty. This ambiguity makes a positive outcome doubtful and leaves you dangling on the line. It appears to me, from hard cold experience, that some women want to have it both ways: to keep you on ice until they sort out if the boyfriend is a keeper and to keep you in the dugout to later swing in their place as desired. Imagine the contorted look of incredulity on these women's faces when I tell them that I won't wait until they give the mysterious other man the heave-ho. I am more than a little pissed at myself for agreeing to either of these dates, which I can now add turned out as expected for reasons very much within the spirit of this tequila-laden story.

All said and done, I simply wish she hadn't needed to throw up. I wish we could have kissed, shared our feelings about life, love and the pursuit of happiness, discuss whether it's Richard Ford or Pete Dexter[37], Stevie Ray Vaughn or Jimi Hendrix, Basquiat or the Dutch Masters[38], Silver Oak or Camus Cabernet,[39] Santorini or Corfu[40], Nigirisushi, makisushi or Sashimi,[41] Yerba Mate'[42] or espresso, or what's at the far end of the electromagnetic spectrum, you know, a world of such minor details like that. Is that too much to ask? Despite the above, I know it will work out some day. I have faith. I can learn. She will arrive. I will find "The One."

Epilogue

While indeed all of the above is true, this happened many years ago. "The One" did appear. Her name is Laura. It is funny how it all worked out. Eventually, I gave up. I got to a point in my life where on a Friday night at 10:30 p.m. I would much rather have been alone at home in peace than out on a date. I left the single world to itself. I had had enough of the games and wasted time. I quit trying. I decided to "Let go and let God" (Psalms 46:10) and trust that He would provide me a mate and best friend when it was right and in His time. He did. Funny enough, it happened in a Starbucks when I was simply minding my own business. Out of the corner of my eye, I spotted a devastatingly cute woman giving me the big eye. She was ¡en fuego! It was all over and yet just beginning.

Laura and I were married on Ngemelis Island in Palau, with our bare feet in the sand surrounded by our daughters, close friends and a circle of coconuts. Aside from the caves I have described elsewhere in *Dead Stuck*, the rock islands of Palau are a wonder of God that must be seen at least once in a lifetime. We still get misty eyed when we watch the wedding video. As weddings go, it was an original. Aside from the Bible readings and self-written vows, each of our children wrote out what they wanted to say at our wedding. Their reflections on love, our marriage and how they saw our new family was as honest and heartfelt as it could have been. It was the best day of my life.

For the record, we all say and do things when young that we would never do again as we get older. Such would describe many of the things I did or thought when I was younger and related in the story above. But we get too fast old and too late smart. (Wolfgang Mieder 316) Stay tuned... Viva la Penis!

Part 2

Setting the Kids Free

A Christmas Letter to Remember

"I have found the best way to give advice to your children is to find out what they want then advise them to do it." (Krieger 270)

Henry S. Truman (1884 – 1972) (The Presidents)

My identical twin daughters, Alana and Bianca were born November 2, 1987, 10 weeks prematurely. At birth, they weighted 2 and ½ pounds and were 14 inches long. My pinky finger was as big as one of their legs. I went through my endodontic training from 1988 to 1991 when they were infants. This letter was written and intended to be a keepsake for them at Christmas, 2004. They were 17 at the time. It started as a half page and grew quickly. While it has been edited for grammar and punctuation, its substance remains intact.

Many medical professionals, to one degree or another, experience burnout. It is unproductive to cite a laundry list of life and business stresses that can lead to this outcome. We all encounter in our work and personal lives what seem at the time to be unsolvable problems, unbearable stresses and insurmountable challenges. Life offers us options for change, self-improvement and greater satisfaction regardless of where we stand at the moment. What matters is not the stresses and failures, they will be always be there. What is important is what we do with them. In some detail, the Christmas letter provides the girls a road map to the decisions they will have to make and the abundant possibilities their lives hold before them. It speaks volumes to the mistakes I've made and how I pray that they will learn from them.

Dear Alana and Bianca,

My intention has always been to raise happy, intelligent, hard working and loving young women who had before them all the possibilities they deserve. You have turned out to be the fine young women I had hoped for. I am very proud of you.

Gazing at the tubes, ventilators and IVs in you on the day you were born in the pediatric ICU at the Stanford Hospital, I watched in awe at the miracle of your arrival. I never asked the doctors for your chances of survival. I had an abiding faith that you would live. You are every bit a miracle to me now. I am still in awe. Gazing at you as innocent newborns, I possessed what I suspect is the unspoken and universal belief of all new parents. I vowed to myself I would do everything in my power to protect you. As time progressed, the simplicity of this notion has evaporated. Parenting turned out to be much more complex than cushioning life's blows for you. I have learned a lot with you along this journey. Among many things, I've learned that life's hardships are vital for your growth and that spoiling you is far more destructive than having high expectations.

As I thought about what to give you this Christmas, I decided on something personal, a letter that you can carry forward as you leave home. On my deathbed, I do not wish to leave anything unspoken between us. Keep this. Refer to it often. I hope this letter helps you find peace and abundance and keeps you from needless misery. Nothing is held back on these pages. It's the best I have to give you.

Know that I am behind you in all things as you finish high school and leave home. Understand though that my love and support does not necessarily translate to financial backing for everything you may want or even need, now or in the future. Love demands that a parent stand aside at some point in their children's lives and let them go forward without interference. You must learn to walk on your own two feet. I will not impose myself into your business, most especially when I am not asked. Personal accountability and responsibility in all aspects of your life start right here, right now. I do not expect nor desire for you to be like me or to live for my approval. You are free to become the women you wish. You will not disappoint me if my advice goes unheeded. You will own your successes. You will own your failures. Your future is yours, not mine.

I gave you my best. That said, I have certainly made mistakes while raising you, though these mistakes pale in comparison to the things that I have done right. As I do not judge you, it is not productive for you to judge me. Judging anyone, except tyrants, rapists and axe murderers, is problematic. Get caught in the "Jaws of Life"[43] (get married, have a career, pay taxes, see the world) and you will find that life is not simple. We are not and do not have to be the masters of the universe. Let God judge. Let he who is without sin cast the first stone (John 8.7). Holding in anger or bitterness about something I did or did not do to you years ago or even yesterday keeps us apart. I forgive you for the things you have done that have hurt me. Please forgive me in return.

Mistakes: Gifts Wrapped in Shit

Let us begin this letter with mistakes. They are a phenomenal teacher. You, like me, will make a boatload of them. What adult has not? With perfect hindsight, mistakes are powerful signs pointing us to where we can be better human beings. Mistakes are gifts that have been exquisitely wrapped in shit! As Nietzsche said, "What does not kill him makes him stronger." (Nietzsche 207) Anyone can steer the ship in clear weather. When the sea of life rocks, our true qualities surface. Brian DesRoches[44] taught me that mistakes and their aftermath cause people to "change, get sick, or die." Change implies learning. We change because we realize there is a better way than ours. Getting emotionally sick, with its accompanying physical symptoms, despite how hard we may try to ignore them, tells us that something is wrong and needs desperate attention. Death only happens to those who continue to plunge headlong into something that, despite the warning signs, will clearly kill them.

When your approach to an issue fails, change course. Do not stubbornly remain tied to bankrupt strategies. A wise friend once told me, "If you always do what you always did, you will always get what you always got." (qtd. in Keyes 99) If you do not like your circumstances (marriage, money, career, where you live), don't complain. Change it. Be proactive. When something is wrong, do not hope for change. Move with love intention, and forethought toward your desired outcome. The worst approach is to stay put in a festering debacle with soiled pants. Pay the price, do the hard work. Never step over the trash.

No matter how smart, beautiful, talented and rich you may become, you have much to learn. We all do. It has been said that there is what you know, what you don't know and what you don't know that you don't know (read that a few times so it sinks in!). Much in this life we don't know that we don't even know. Improving our lives, solving problems and growing into greater health are a function of embracing continual evolution at every level. There are no shortcuts to this work. As long as you are breathing, you will be learning, changing and making mistakes. Otherwise you are just marking time until death.

Setting the Kids Free

Intuitive Living: The Two Worlds

Searching beyond a superficial understanding and appreciation of events and daily life reveals truth and reality. A surface level view is often misleading. Things are rarely as they first appear. Look into the deeper subtext of everything. Observe below the surface. Attempt to see what is really being played out around you. An honest assessment will help you avoid many of life's icebergs. If you anticipate your challenges, many titanic problems that would otherwise bedevil you can often be foreseen. Search the horizon (the superficial view of events) carefully and do not forget that 90 percent of the iceberg is below the water (the true reality). Knowing the iceberg's full dimensions can help you steam around it safely.

People have universal struggles. You will have the same challenges. You have no immunity. There will be different actors, different stages, but life's dances and dramas and tragedies are replayed incessantly. One such reoccurring sinkhole, out of a universe of examples, is the man who tires of his nagging wife and takes a mistress. Perhaps in this scenario, the husband never intended to be faithful. The mistress has no direction of her own. She is temporarily thrilled by the affair because of the transient power or attention received. The wife in this play hates her role. She is both bored and unloved by her husband. Divorce in this triangle is inevitable. Does this sound familiar? It has been and will continue to be played out endlessly. The finale is already known. Be not the husband, wife or the mistress.

Appearances are indeed deceiving. While outwardly a person might appear tranquil, their soul may be ravaged. Aside from our intuition, we are not mind readers and we may not know the true intentions of another until we have a proven track record with them. Feelings are fleeting. Acting on feelings is dangerous. Act on the bedrock, below the feelings. Act on that which is proven true by time, not on impulse. Beware of unspoken agendas. Some people will attempt to get close to you for their own gain. While on the surface it may seem as though they wish to be your friend, perhaps nothing could be further from the truth. Your best chance at finding friendship with another will come when neither of you stands to gain financially or otherwise from the exchange. My most satisfying friendships have come from those relationships that are long term and take place where nothing is at stake. In essence, where we are in relationship only because we enjoy each other's company.

Know the back-story before you make decisions of consequence or form indelible impressions of the world beyond yourself. Think beyond the headlines. Virtually everything you read, watch and see advertised is biased with an agenda toward the position of the author. Understanding these dynamics can prevent your manipulation. Some will seek to use you for their gain, be they politicians, advertisers or news sources. *Caveat emptor*. Let the buyer beware. I am a great believer in Ronald Reagan's famous quote "Trust, but verify." (Sherry Sontag 259)

Hope for the best, plan for the worst and walk with your head up to see what is coming at and occurring around you. Ask questions. Human misery is fed from the same unending and yet highly predictable streams of behavior. Expecting people and history to be different in the future is wishful and naive. The world has its share of dreamers; those who believe that if we all sat around the campfire and sang "Kumbaya" that evil would not touch us. Such dreamers refuse to believe that evil exists or they blindly choose to ignore it. They deny any reality other than the one they believe should exist. This mindset is dangerous in the extreme if for no other reason than with it, we withhold the truth from ourselves. Even the most superficial study of history is rife with examples of the struggle for power and resources and its violent consequences at a global and personal level. Peace will reign when Jesus comes back. Not a second before. The Bible says that there will be wars and rumors of war until the end of time (Matt 24: 6-7). It is true. History repeats itself. To have a comprehensive understanding of this life, its meanings and possibilities, you must assess what is really being presenting to you in the way of threats and opportunities at any given moment and not simply hoping that everything will work out on its own.

As adults, how many of us would like to take a decision back five minutes or five years after we made it? If we were honest with ourselves, would we deny with 20/20 hindsight that we saw warning signs and chose to plough on through the red light at high speed into an otherwise preventable personal wreck? Present events have a myriad of unseen future meanings and consequences. Present details, even those that appear to be inconsequential, when linked to a future outcome, often demonstrate that the first event was a direct foreshadowing to what eventually became reality.

Appreciating things as they really are and not as you wish them to be can allow you to walk around the threats and make the most of your opportunities. Knowing where to go and how to get there in life stems, in part, from knowing what is really in front of and behind us, in essence, to know the truth about the world around us as we move toward our goals. See what is really being played out around you in the various theaters of your life. Who means you well? Who means you harm? Who is trying to use you for their advantage? Who drains you? Who energizes you? Who has consistently told you the truth? Who has lied? This list of such questions is long, but much of what will challenge you in this life is entirely predictable by learning from the past and seeing, interpreting and admitting truth in the present. If you will look for the right answers you will find them. If you do not find the right answers, the wrong ones will most certainly find you.

Some would argue that everything is open to interpretation and that there are no absolutes, no true reality, no right or wrong. There are shades of gray on some things, but ultimately right is right and wrong is wrong. Those with a sliding values scale tilt the ledger toward their personal profit and gain, always.

This duality of awareness has another dimension and application. We are most happy and fulfilled when our perceptions match reality. In essence, we have the potential to be most happy when we see things as they really are, both in the larger world and within ourselves. For example, if I wish to have something I do not have or wish to be something I am not, I am in tension. My peace and joy vanishes. Living our inner truth in our outer lives is difficult. It means not conforming and saying no to peer pressure. It will bring ridicule and exclusion. I have reached a point in my life where I care not if I am ridiculed or excluded. I hope this for you. Honest self-reflection is not easy and will not come quickly. Be patient with yourselves when things go wrong. Your mistakes and misfortunes are indeed all "gifts wrapped in shit." Take the long-term view; it can be months or years before the gift appears from under the stink. Have faith, keep your perspective; the gift will emerge in time.

Let peace begin with me.

Choose your battles carefully. Conflict is rarely productive. If humanly possible, avoid it. In human and financial terms, it is very expensive. Irrespective of how right you may be, conflict and personal turmoil steals your peace of mind. Rarely does confrontation bear fruit, only lingering trauma. Walk around difficult people. Walk around unsolvable problems that are out of your control. There are many of these half covered sinkholes in life. The painful truth is that if people wanted to behave differently toward you in a given situation, they already would. You are not going to change them by telling them they are wrong, suing or attacking them.

An ounce of prevention, versus a pound of cure, will go a long way toward achieving and maintaining peace in your kingdom. Keep your dignity. Never be a doormat. Think before you speak. Walk away if it is not crucially important. Ask yourself, "Is this going to matter in 10 years?" Speak slowly when conflict is in the air. Lower your voice. Control your breathing. Step away until you can be rational. Pick up the phone before you default to lawyers or go on the offensive. Sometimes making a small concession initially leads to a far greater reward later in time, money and stomach lining compared to the cost of engagement. Ask questions first; shoot later and then only if there is no other option.

In conflict, people default to pointing the finger. Be part of the solution and not focused on placing blame. "Be a fountain, not a drain." (Musial 211) The answer to bring resolution in any conflict is always there if you ask the right questions of yourself, your advisors and the other party. Questions such as: "What are my options in this situation?" "How much of the blame do I own for this problem?" "What is the best (and worst) possible outcome to engagement in this problem?" "Is this worth my energy, time and money?" "What will ultimately cost me more money and time, settling now, walking away, or sinking my teeth into it?" "Is my pride fueling this conflict?" "What do I really hope to gain out of this?" and "Why do I want or need to win this conflict?" can all go far toward bringing perspective in an adversarial environment.

The older I get, the easier it has become for me to let go of petty insults, dishonesty and injustices. I cannot change the behavior of others, but I can control my reaction to all of these things. Taking from the spirit of Ghandi, I can be the change I wish to see in the world. (qtd. in Keyes 75) Hanging on to every offense, perceived or real, is an immensely heavy burden to carry. Just let it be and move on. I have never won an argument. It's a safe bet that you won't win many either. The best you can do is to associate yourself with like-minded people and move forward with those who support you while maintaining an open mind and a respect for the other side of anything. This is called tolerance. People change because they want to, not by force. Many people will change behaviors or positions in conflict only when confronted with such enormous pain that they cannot bear further suffering. They are not going to change their behavior because you asked them to, no matter how right you are.

Bear in mind that, more often than not, people default to a position that either makes them money or saves them money. Follow the money. Some people's future actions can be read like a book by observing who will profit from a given outcome. While a sad and cynical commentary, it has been my life experience where money or resources hang in the balance. All of this said, in rare moments, you may need to fight. You may have to make instant decisions in difficult circumstances. Knowing when to walk away and when to go to war is an art form. Bear in mind that once it commences, conflict must be seen through. Do not slide in cleats up unless you are willing to break their ankles.[45] Be right before you start. Have the tools to finish. Some people are simply wrong and mean to hurt you. Wisdom lies in knowing when to slide in or pull out of the tackle. Save yourself a world of hurt. Avoid conflict with others if at all possible; the ankles you save will likely be your own.

Fear, Procrastination and Doing Your Best

What is past is prologue. If it has happened before, it will happen again. Work hard, play hard, life is short. Take a lot of time off. You can never have enough health or time. Aside from faith in God, these are your most precious personal resources. Do not waste either through laziness or procrastination. Avoid preventable stress. If you have three months to do a term paper, do not wait until the last week to begin. Waiting leaves no wiggle room for unexpected opportunities or added tasks. Peace of mind is a function of having the time to enjoy life's simple pleasures as others may spin in chaos. Free time is created through personal effectiveness and organization. Being proactive stands out in Mt. Rushmore's boldness in contrast to people who flitter about like headless chickens, reacting to events rather than directing them. You are the writer, producer and videographer of your life story. Make it what you truly want it to be.

Some live in a land called "hope" that their problems will magically disappear. They avoid entirely what they know must be done in their own lives, their families and in the world beyond. This procrastination will never bring personal or professional growth. Face your challenges head on until they are resolved. The pain of correct action is always less than the pain and consequence of waiting to deal with a situation that forces resolution upon you. Said differently, hoping that a situation will improve and waiting until others make a decision for you is never as satisfactory as being the architect of the solution yourself.

"God helps those who help themselves." (Keyes 79) Work first and play second. You will have infinitely more time to play this way. Work creates the conditions that provide safety and security. Always leave something extra in your tank. Flying at full throttle without reserve power for emergencies is risky. The flip side is that you will not know what you are capable of unless you push yourself to the limit. Your confidence will rise as you learn your capabilities. Unfortunately, the converse is also true when you fail and foolishly waste precious resources in the process. Whatever you do, be as strong in the 85th minute of the match as you were in the 5th.[46]

Friends

People come and go. Friends remain, no matter what. If you get through life with one or two true lifelong friends, you are rich beyond measure. Real friendship is a proven quantity that is present only after the resolution of differences with a resulting deeper connection. If the relationship is not battle tested by disagreement, the person is an acquaintance. If you remain connected and in deeper relationship to someone after conflict, you have something.

Rapid decisions about people can easily miss the mark. The person you thought was your friend can easily stab you in the back when it is to their gain. A person who has stood off and been indifferent might just come to your aid in your most dire time of need, even when you have no indication they care. Do not burn bridges; you will need them when you must retreat. Seek friendship. Open your heart to others. Listen to people. Look for opportunities to help and heal. Expect nothing in return. Give freely. At the end of the day, have the blind faith your love will be returned when and where you need it most. It will.

You will meet energy vampires. Be prepared. Their problems are not yours, not even for a second. While thankfully few, there are those who would suck dry every ounce of your spirit and possibly finances through a twisted manipulation of your love and good nature. No matter how much you do for these people, it is not enough. They are never at peace. In the give and take equation, they only know how to take. They give always expecting more in return. Figuratively, energy vampires can put a tap into you and turn the handle on and off at will if the dynamic of the relationship is not appreciated. The more kind and successful you are, the more of these people you will attract. Dad's advice is simple. For your own self-preservation, no matter how challenging at the moment, this personality type is to be avoided at all costs.

Remove toxic people from your life. Do not walk on pins and needles around such people. Politely but firmly tell them you cannot have them in your life no matter who they are. Stake out appropriate boundaries to insulate yourself from unhealthy behavior. Keep your relationships at a level that have mutual benefit. Some people think they can manage abusive relationships and remain in them out of a misguided sense of duty or love. Families that allow child molesters and wife beaters to remain as a member of the larger family unit without intervention or consequence are an example. This is dysfunctional and unhealthy in the extreme. The loving and intelligent thing to do is to avoid being sucked into such situations entirely.

Money

Live in balance financially. Money itself is neither good nor bad, it just is. There is no greater way to be free than for you to manage money well. On the one hand, there is no faster way for you to be enslaved than to use it irresponsibly. People's actions around money are the truest indication of their personal integrity. Bank on it. Someone who is miserly about money is telling you what they value. It is not likely to be you.

Anything really worth having is worth sweating, working and ultimately dying for, otherwise its just stuff. You are going out of this world in your birthday suit. The rest is window dressing. He who dies with the most toys still dies. While this is true, money is important. People who say otherwise are usually the same ones who are worried because they do not have enough. Money is one measure of your work ethic and self-discipline. Buy what you need and not what you want. The "stuff" mentioned above becomes a loaded wheelbarrow you have to push through life. Think twice before you buy anything. Life's wheelbarrow is easily loaded down with mortgages, private school tuition, boats, car payments, clothes, jewelry and expensive meals. The more assets you acquire, the more the assets acquire you to manage, monitor and protect them. The ugly truth that "rich" people will rarely say aloud is that someone, somewhere is always trying to take advantage of them. Ask a celebrity about outstretched hands grabbing at them for money and favors. The progressive income tax structure in the United States is also testament to this. Rich people pay more as a percentage of their income than lower earners. While it's easy to sell this concept to politicians and the wider public, at some point it kills the incentive to work and penalizes innovation. Tell a contractor you are a doctor, and see what happens to the cost of the project.

Dead Stuck

Spend less than you make. You deserve nice things (we all do), but if you cannot afford something, don't buy it. Pay cash, never use credit for long term financing except for your house mortgage. Irresponsible credit card use and materialistic consumption are a form of modern serfdom. The world wants into your wallet. There are armies of clever people who have devised innumerable methods to separate you from the fruits of your labor. Will you love the drink, clothes, perfume or meal that you buy today in six months? Will you remember it in five years? Chances are you will remember only because you might still be paying for it. At the end of the day, you can always get by with less. Start now.

Life's Purpose

Be focused in college. Move toward a career and a life about which you are fiercely passionate. Move toward a vocation that ultimately helps others. In contrast, neglecting your studies and lacking purpose is the road to unfulfilled and aimless servitude. Changing careers in your 30s or 40s is like turning around an aircraft carrier on the open ocean. It is slow and takes a wide berth. I am glad I studied in high school, college, dental school and residency. I wasn't sexy. I wasn't cool. Your dad was a nerd's nerd. This study meant a lot of nights in the library. The payoff was that it gave me a freedom your grandparents could only dream of. Be able to go to Hawaii or Europe once in your life (and call that enough) or to be able to wake up and see the sunrise off the summit of Mt. Fuji, dive the WWII wrecks in the Truk Lagoon, trek above Everest base camp, see Manchester United at Old Trafford, go on Safari in South Africa, wake up on the beach in Sri Lanka or sea kayak in the Abel Tasman sea. The choice is yours. What do you want for yourself and your children? A passionate "yes" means putting your heart and soul into your work. Anything other than unconditional commitment means going without these perks. One choice isn't necessarily better than another, but what is more important than knowing where you are going in your life, why, how and with whom?

You will not be given back one second of your life. The breath you just exhaled is gone forever. Where you take your last breath in life and how you take it stems in large part from what you do with your life right now, this very minute. What is important is not how much money or power you have, but rather that you be content and fulfilled with the path you devote yourself to. In essence, that you are happy with what you have. Being happy with what you have and not wishing for more is a cornerstone of personal fulfillment. You will never have enough money to feel entirely secure. Be happy with what you have and work toward improving what needs changing in your life. Be content with that. Do not keep wishing for more. Longing for more robs you of happiness both in the present and future. As human beings, we will never feel truly secure because we know we are going to die. My security comes from my faith in God and the promise of heaven. In essence, death is not my end, just a change in form. This is liberating.

Mastery

Mastering anything takes time and practice. Mastery is a never-ending journey. The rare individual is a true master at more than one thing. To be good at any one thing requires an intense long-term effort and constant practice. For people to pay you for something beyond simple labor, you must have a skill to sell. For the master of a skill, there will always be demand. For others, their fate, especially economically, will always be subject to the winds of change. Whatever you do, be the best at it that you possibly can. If you choose a career that you are passionate about, it is not work. Your passions now are a strong clue as to what you should do with your career. If your career helps others, the easier it will be to wholeheartedly devote yourself to it.

Being Happy in the Here and Now

Life is not fair. Sometimes the bread falls with the buttered side down. Pain and disappointment are part of life. Do not get too excited when you win or too down when you lose. Unless you are dead, you will always have a chance to come back and play another day. Be gracious when you win and when you lose. Happiness and joy spring from understanding what disappointment and failure feel like. No matter how rich and talented you are, it is not possible to have one without the other. Everyone has a cross to bear. No one has it easy. The Buddhists call this experience of journeying through life, "samsara." (Bhikkhu) It is an inescapable fact. Bitching about others, bad luck or circumstances beyond your control is entirely unproductive.

When not on the mountaintop, some people spend much of their time complaining about the valleys. There are many dips in this life. We spend precious little time in our lives where everything is just right. We spend a great deal of time moving from one mountaintop (or perceived benchmark) to another. If we cannot be happy when things are not going well, life is a long slog. Predict the future by making the future you want. Knowing exactly where you want to go is a very strong step to making it happen. Belief and decision about the end of your life's journey gives you direction. Without this compass, you are cast adrift on the open ocean in a rowboat. Unless you are Captain Bligh[47] and a master seaman, you will be very lucky to land where you should.

You will make three seminal choices in your life: 1) Your faith 2) Whom you marry 3) Your chosen profession. Get these decisions right, and you will have happiness in great measure despite life's challenges. Get these wrong, and simple decisions like being married and choosing to get pregnant become Herculean tasks in the event of a toxic divorce.

Always take the long view, never the short-term gain. What seeds you plant today will be the reality you grow down the line. Sooner than you realize, a look in the mirror will reveal gray hair, wrinkles and sags. Beauty is cured by time and gravity. You will not live forever. Relish every day. Even at the worst of times, "Every day above ground is a good day."(Scarface) Thank God every morning that He woke you up. It is only by the grace of God that we have our many blessings and that we are here. The world does not spin around you. You are a part of it. When you are long gone, it will continue as it always has. Others will carry on. While you are on earth, create something that has great value to yourself and those around you. What will have value to you on your deathbed? Will it be expensive toys or will it be happy memories and your family looking at you with love? Decide now what it is you want on your tombstone. From this day forward, decide what you stand for. Sort out unmistakably who you are. Do not believe the hype that you can have it all. You cannot. Choose now what you want to pick up along the way, what you will leave behind and what you want to end this life with.

Never let the critics and doubters get under your skin or influence your decisions. No matter who you are, no matter what you have, no matter how right you are, there will always be someone standing in your way and slagging you off. Expect criticism, especially if you dedicate yourself to something of great value to the world. Any task performed well is a blessing to everyone around you. There are innumerable ways to help others. Every single day, God gives us ways to contribute. You do not need to be Mother Theresa, St. Francis of Assisi or Gandhi to move the world. Learn from their spirit, but remember that just listening when it's inconvenient is an act of mercy to the person being heard. Know when to speak and when to be silent. You cannot learn by speaking. In a world where people spend inordinate amounts of time shouting at each other divisively, listening is a powerful way to be compassionate.

Faith

I am absolutely convicted there is a creator. I call that creator God. Nature is too complex, abundant and resplendent for me to accept that random energy; time and mathematical chance brewed our world and universe out of the primordial sludge. I envision, feel and experience God as the Father, Son and the Holy Ghost. Intuitively, it makes sense to me that people of all faiths feel, experience and worship the same divine force even though we may call Him by different names.

I have innumerable questions for and about God. For example, the Bible says the world was created in seven days. The Bible is the infallible word of God. How can that be when the evidence for evolution over the millennia is irrefutable? Despite not having all the answers, I am comfortable with incongruity and seeming contradictions. I believe unconditionally. I pray to God and with an open and obedient heart for His guidance in my life.

My faith both guides me and gives me hope. A world without God's guiding hand, where what we know in our physical world is all there is, presents me with a frightening and futile proposition. Man's track record at sustaining the planet and loving his neighbor is at best mediocre. The cutting of the last tree on Easter Island[48] and the Holocaust are but two small examples in a multitude of human abuses of our world and each other. If no heaven or hell exists, if there is no God, there is little if any reason to moderate our behavior. Without a higher power, why not just do whatever we want and ignore our fellow man? To whom do we have to answer? A world without God is one where might makes right and any inherent obligations we might have to others or them to us are not at all clear to me.

Rationality, logic and secular values, the absence of God, have not proven throughout history to be a sustainable way forward. Depending on the goodness of man or man's higher cognitive powers to compel him to coexist peacefully is a myth. It has never happened. It will never happen. Religious wars throughout history were fought precisely because those who fought them did not have faith and God's love to guide them. Their actions have nothing to do with religion or God. These leaders and groups engaged in war precisely because they disobeyed the word of God unless they acted in self-defense.

What's this all got to do with you? Some people have oodles of excuses about why religion isn't relevant to them and how we have evolved and should believe in science, technology, rationality and logic. The pervasive message from the non-believing world is that anyone who believes in God, especially the Christian manifestation of God, is deluded. What is interesting is that many of these same people never publically criticize Islam, Hinduism, Buddhism, or the Native American spiritual traditions, among others. Many of these same people preach tolerance outwardly, but if anything are fiercely intolerant of everyone who does not believe what they do. Much the same could be said of the far political right and left in America today. The above notwithstanding, there are many tolerant and immensely kind non-believers. Some of the most "Christian" people I know in demeanor and action are non-believers! Alternatively, some of the most judgmental people I have ever met call themselves "Christian." It is neither for you or me to judge anyone, believer or non-believer. Either way, this is relevant in your spiritual walk. You will face obstacles in searching for God as the popular culture emerging in America today generally does not support belief. In many ways you will be on your own, except to the degree that you surround yourself with like-minded people who can support you and help you grow in faith. Some people will ridicule you, either to your face or behind your back, for your belief. I ignore this. You can as well.

Separate God from some of His believers. Do not blame God for the acts of a few of His followers. With all faiths, God is God; the churches and religions of this world are man made. Organized religion throughout the ages has, at times, tragically and violently used the shield of God for man's hateful designs. Seek the love, mercy, grace and forgiveness of God and ignore the man made flaws of any church. Keep your sights set on the presence of God in your life, ignore the politics of religion. God is perfect, man far less so. Man's politics and what is done in God's name often has little to do with the good news of the Bible.

Love and forgiveness are the only way forward. While simple in word, these are often monumentally challenging in action. Being Christian involves a delicate dance that we undertake as believers to both live in the world and yet not be of the world. The world will tempt you with sin and excess. You need the conviction to ignore what the world offers that can poison your body and spirit. Walking away from temptation can be very hard to do. It is not easy to love those who hate you, to turn the other cheek or to walk away from illicit profit or pleasure when offered. Make the loving choice, especially when it is the most painful and difficult option open to you. Your flesh and spirit will flourish. You will be at peace. The converse is true. Every act not motivated by love will drain you of fulfillment. The cumulative effect of these decisive choices in your life will define your spiritual health and ultimately determine if you are happy in your heart. If the decision is loving and honors life, it is the right decision and comes from God. These moments, where we must chose between right and wrong, where seemingly no one is watching, are the true tests of our character. No matter what you do, no matter how sure you are that you will get away with it, it never plays out that way. We never get away with it. Our misdeeds always catch up to us. Do the right thing, even when it hurts. Your heart and soul will be light, your worries few and your spirit free. The peace you will own as a result is priceless.

God will answer you when you ask questions of Him, in His time, not yours. Search to find the spirit of God. The keyword is "search" as it relates to faith. Deepening spiritual health does not happen by accident. As you search, through the Holy Ghost, God will speak to you. Know that ultimately faith requires obedience, a submission to a higher power beyond you. Your present needs, wishes and problems are not the center of the universe. Don't get wrapped up in your own dramas and issues. It's not all about you. It's not all about me. It's about all of us, collectively as a planet, with God's loving hand under us. We are all part of something much larger. As people of many races, colors and faiths, God calls us to place kindness before anger, peace before conflict and love before hate. It is just that simple. Believing that God has a plan for our lives unshackles us. We do not need to worry about every detail of our present or future needs. We can sleep in the assurance of God's promise that He will provide for us. He does. We do not need to keep score or worry about what tomorrow may bring. At the end of the day, the best is all we can do. And the best we can do is to love without holding back. If you really think about all of your problems, you will find at some level, that you or someone else did not love the way that they could or should have. Love is the final answer to all questions. Ultimately, it is the only response to what confronts us.

Whether or not we choose to accept it, we all worship something, whether that is God, ourselves or other idols. Whatever we focus on primarily over the long term is our object of worship. What is fascinating to me is that people continue to worship what has already been proven empty and powerless and yet somehow expect their affection for the activity or substance to provide a different outcome. It never does.

To what will you give your time, attention and ultimately your soul? Can you sleep peacefully if your spirit is troubled? Does not everything you take in, physically, spiritually and cognitively, affect your peace of mind? Are not those things to which you give yourself over the long term your "God?" The answer is a resounding "Yes!" Whatever you focus on and consume at any given moment is your master. Your collective life experience is the sum total of these innumerable moments. Is the object of your devotion enriching or sinking your spirit? If you find yourself unhappy, ask yourself to what you have given yourself over? What end result has your object of devotion provided you? Where has it taken you? Are not earthly pursuits of pleasure and profit a series of oases that eventually dry up and vanish, ending upon our passing from this world, vacuous and unfulfilled? Devotion to any idol (money, sex, power) that is not our core purpose in life and ultimately based in God's love is much like adoring a rock star who does not know we exist. At some point the star fades, the fantasy ends and we are left empty, having devoted immense amounts of ourselves, most often self destructively, to an illusion.

Be Decisive

When in doubt, think three times before you act on something of vital importance. Make sure your head, heart and gut are aligned to the right decision. Then go for it with reckless abandon. To not act is to live in uncertainty and fear. Dolares Ibárruri was right, 'It is better to die on your feet than to live on your knees." (qtd. in Fred R. Shapiro 380) It is better to exhaust yourself being all that God intended than dying anonymously. Never follow the crowd. The maddening crowd is often like the buffalo that were run off a cliff by the Indians in the Badlands of South Dakota to feed the tribes. Because everyone does something is never a measuring stick for what is right for you. Your friends might start to marry and have children at 28. Their "biologic clock" or other rationales are irrelevant. Wait patiently until such decisions are correct for you.

I understand both the conventional wisdom and the road less traveled. My instinct has always been to walk away from the crowd. Groups of people (families, neighborhoods, countries) often have beliefs and conventional wisdom that may in fact be unproductive, unhealthy or simply wrong. "Group think" dogma is often specious. Be yourself, not one of "them." In time, "they" will be gone from your life and you will remain. We live with the consequences of our actions, whether committed as part of a group or alone. Never bow to peer pressure. A boatload of hip drug users from 1960s ended up dead, disabled or a shadow of their true selves, the price paid for being "cool" in the day. While some of them would probably do it again, many would not. Ignore what is fashionable today. Opt for quintessence, those values and qualities that have timeless appeal, for me best spoken as "Love your neighbor as yourself." (Matthew 22:37-39)

Happiness

I am absolutely convinced that we determine, in large measure, our degree of happiness in this life and we are not acted upon by fate or destiny. Our future is written neither in the stars, nor in the happenstance of wishful thinking. Rather it is written in the blood and guts of everyday life where each belief we accept as true manifests itself as an action, even if the result of that action is evident years on from germination of the concept in our heads. The things we believe, what we hold in our hearts, the values we cling to become the actions we take, whether these actions enslave us to unhealthy habits or alternatively allow us to live with joy and passion.

For some, the game is over before it is ever played. Focused just on the here and now, without forethought or reflection, there is little possibility of change or a better future. How many of us carry a silent millstone around our necks that reminds us how unattractive and unintelligent we are? How many of us dwell on unproductive questions, such as "Why does this always happen to me?" or "Why am I never good enough?" More helpful questions might be: "Where am I now?" "How did I get here?" "What actions can I take today that will change my future?" or "What voice do I hear guiding me forward?" "Where do I really want to be?" "Who am I?"

Do the unhappy so cherish their problems that they wish to live bound by them until death? No one would answer "Yes" to this question. But why do we see the same choices made to repeat unproductive patterns that complete a broken existence with severed relationships, self-inflicted poor health and lack of abundance? How many of us will die lonely because we were unwilling to submit to another in a committed relationship? How many have been hurt in the past and opt to treat relationships as a game instead of having a loving and deepening interaction with another?

Loneliness is a quiet, tragic epidemic. Some men value fishing, college sports and other hobbies more than their wives. Some women value their freedom more than the love they simultaneously crave. In either case, irrespective of gender differences, there is clearly a decision by some to close themselves off from love through clutching to a set of behaviors that hold the individual away from the love they desire. This separation away from love is a choice. Love invested in the right person can be immensely empowering, and, alternatively, in the wrong person it will choke one almost to death. Knowing both whom to love and how to love are inextricably linked. Much like the seed that must be placed on fertile ground and tended, love must be given in the right relationship to prosper. This brings us to boys.

Men, Sex, Marriage and Relationships.

You are ready for a happy marriage when you could care less, not a minute before. Your best chance at marital happiness lies in your being happy and at peace with yourself first. Only then can you fully give and receive love.

Most people want what they want and generally do not change. What a prospective mate says they want and what they really want is often different. Some may not really even know what they want even though they say they do. Expecting change or hoping that things will get better or different in time is fruitless. 99.9 percent of the time, if someone is drinking excessively, doing drugs or is careless with money, it is a safe bet that these things will get worse. It is foolhardy to be physically, mentally, emotionally and financially vulnerable to another person's weakest link in marriage in the naïve hope that things will improve.

In human relationships, blind love does not conquer all. "Follow your heart" is the advice of an artist. "Follow your head" is the advice of a banker. "Follow your gut" is the advice of a gambler. Follow them all, which is the advice of a father who loves you. All said differently, marriage is a blend of love, power, business, intense emotions and childhood experience that has the ability to make you most fully human and alive and also the power to make you wish you were dead. As it relates to "love" and "marriage" the hitch is there is no magic formula. There is no one right way. If there were a formula we would all be following it like happy bunnies. You can be the most loving person on the planet and get hammered in a marriage if your love is not tempered with common sense. Align your head, heart and gut together and make the best decision you can. If you have doubts, do not marry the person.

There is never a reason to hurry marriage. Assertions like "This is my last chance at love," "He is the best I could hope for" and other such platitudes are outward expressions of an inner void. These statements are red flags. Someone thinking in these terms is using a potential mate to fill a need or provide an answer to a problem. None of us can make the world right for another person. Inner peace begins within the individual and moves outward. Some holes of need (lack of self-confidence, poor self-esteem, jealousy) cannot be filled. Having the same faith, goals, means of operating in the world with regard to money, use of time, health and leisure activities create compatibilities. Different faiths, stepchildren or a toxic ex-spouse etc are challenges to intimacy, to one degree or another. While they can be mastered, these problematic issues take a significant amount of the relationship's energy to navigate.

Never be embarrassed to ask hard questions in your relationships. You need to know exactly what cruise you are signing up for. Be cautious of whose advice you take about relationships. Advice is based on the wisdom and experience of the giver. Their advice stems from their marital world, it does not have to be yours. Avoid relationship clichés like "opposites attract." Such pablum has nothing to do with your specific circumstances.

Competence is a huge issue for men. Insult a man's competence at your peril. The first time you break up with a boy, see how he takes it. If he comes back crying, beats down the door or calls repeatedly, do not be surprised and do not answer. Irrespective of how right you may be to end the relationship, you have insulted both his manhood and competence. A man who reacts this way is operating from a position of need. You cannot rescue him. Ideally, the person who is told that a relationship is over should accept it gracefully and move on. The most merciful thing that you can do is to walk away peacefully so that each party can heal, learn and apply the lessons in a better future. For the men who are not keepers it's catch and release, throw them back. These men need to find their own way, without you. It is the most merciful thing you can do both for yourself and them to make a clean break. Spare yourself the exhausting all night conversation with its histrionics and drama. When it's time to end it, kick him to the curb with honesty and finality.

Many is the woman who has fallen for the good looking cowboy who just seems to be a little short on luck, money and love. There are many male archetypes, not just this one (the iconic cowboy), but the clues are there and you need to look very hard at which of these your man might fall into: the macho stud athlete, the academic, Peter Pan, the good ole' boy, etc. While it is always dangerous to generalize, there are patterns in style, substance and the character of men. See the patterns. Bury the rose colored glasses driven by hormonal infatuation. Such infatuation can last for two minutes or two years. The deeper love that most people seek is something tested in the fire of conflict that is absolutely a necessity of any meaningful relationship. Know what you have a hold of; know what they are made of. Push them, test them, and do not fear insulting them through honest questions. Some men can talk a good fight and not deliver. Take a close look before you let a man in your life. Everything about him speaks to his integrity and qualities. If he won't take care of his shoes, he won't take care of you. If he won't stop at one drink when appropriate now, he won't stop at one drink when appropriate later. A man who talks about himself all the time is not the right one. See the truth as it is now, not as you wish it to be in some orgasmic future fantasy. No matter how much you love him or wish things to work out, the decision to marry is not left to hope and chance.

If he has character, he will be forthright and true. A real man will admire your being direct. Look at what he says, not at what he does. Is he generous when he tips? Does he take care of his things without being obsessive? Does he find fault or ask questions first? Does he say "thank you" when you do something for him? Does he open the door for you? Does he praise you when you do something special? Does he stop and face you and listen without distraction when you speak to him? If a man is divorced and has young children, does he call his kids on his nights off? If he cares so little for his kids now, what makes you think he will act differently with the kids you may have together when married? If he makes you pay for dinner when dating, he will count every nickel when you are married. I know a man who used to make his wife pay for two-ply toilet paper out of her own money because he thought one-ply was enough. This behavior speaks of a miserly soul. As expected, with such scorekeeping, the wife was horribly lonely.

Does your prospective prince charming have pornography around the house? Do you accept this? You will never measure up to these sirens. A critic of this advice might respond: "Get real, boys are boys and they have a right to read whatever they want. It harms no one" This comment is a lot like the statement that "Everyone has affairs out of marriage, everyone does it." Not in healthy marriages they don't. I suspect many of these same people spouting this would feel differently if their own daughters were porn stars or their spouses were also having affairs. Your bond with your spouse is a sacred event that is yours alone. Draw clear boundaries, be happy within those and deepen your love in the process. Going to bed with insecurities is one of the pillars of marital discontent. A healthy and happy sex life aside, you are not an accoutrement to your Prince's fantasy world staring in the role of harlot.

Men are not subtle creatures, they do not communicate by Braille. Direct, simple and to the point goes a long way toward getting at whatever needs to be discussed. If his last wife or girlfriend was a "nasty unfeeling bitch" (in his words), what is the chance that you will escape that future tag? How much of a life will you have together if he is away playing softball or fishing every weekend, in essence, absorbed in something other than your family? Will you be expected to keep it all together (your job, the house, the kids) while he fiddles with his hobbies?

Protect yourself. Take baby steps in dating. Make no assumptions. Do not project onto a man the things you think you see or want to feel. The devil comes dressed in nice clothes. He wears neither a red cape nor does he have horns. Go slow when meeting a new boy. Start with coffee. Keep things simple as you get to know each other. You want the man who will wait because he loves and respects you. While generalizing is dangerous, there are a number of men who want a mama to cook, a maid to clean and a whore to sleep with. Crude and not politically correct, but true.

Underestimate the fragility of a man's ego at your peril. Sex is a walloping motivator for men. Date rape and forced sex of all kinds give testimony to the power of sex over men and their need for conquest. This is a tale as old as time. Think of David and Bathsheba from the Bible. (Samuel 2 11.1) David sent Uriah to be killed so he could sleep with the wife. In more subtle ways this happens today.

Suffice it to say, men do not take "no" for an answer gracefully. Sex is a form of sport for many men. Some will do anything to have a woman submit, willingly or otherwise. I have met too many women who have been date raped, drugged, sexually abused and harassed in one form or another for this not to be true. Common sense should guide your actions. Don't drink with men you don't know well and especially not alone with more than one. While you and I cannot change the nature of man and the world should not be this way, you can avoid being victimized by being both street smart and moral. Levels of integrity build on one another. Integrity does not exist in a vacuum. People are not ethical or kind in one area of their lives and unethical in others. Values span the horizon of our lives. Unless he has a "come to Jesus" Epiphany, if a man cheats or lies once, he will again.

Find the compassionate warrior who is willing to tangibly work with you to build a family. These men exist, but finding one takes time. You have a lot of time. You will not be an old maid at 30, or even 35. The right guy might come along early and maybe not, only you will really know. Marriage may or may not be the thing for you. It is your choice. Many is the bride who has stood on the altar telling herself that she is making a mistake only to wish she had waited and listened to her inner voice. Listen to yours.

Personal Effectiveness and the Results of Our Choices

Be decisive, even if it means you will be wrong. Paralysis by analysis is still paralysis. Nothing is permanent except death. Think, plan, decide and act. If something does not work out, get up, dust your shorts off and then try again harder, smarter and longer until you reach your goal. Never ever quit when you feel in your soul that something must be done. Let no force on heaven or earth stop you from being what you were called to be. Go at this life so you can die one day without regret. On your deathbed, you will lament quitting much more than having failed at something.

Do not listen to cynics and doubters. No matter how high you go, there will always, and I mean always, be someone who wants to cut you down and criticize you for being the tall poppy.[49] Take that as a compliment. It means that you threaten them. When people are envious or critical it means you threaten them, in essence, you are doing something right.

Be careful what you put into your body, from drugs to alcohol to men and everything in between. If others take ecstasy before going dancing, ask yourself if this really good for you. Is this who you are? If you have to ask yourself the answer is "no." Just because all the other girls are having sex does not mean it is right for you. Where will they end up? While it is not possible to fully know, chances are it won't be in the place they wanted. Over time, your life will resemble what you do with the temple that is your body and spirit and that includes tattoos! All this said, we can forgive Eric Cantona[50] for the Cherokee chief tattoo! King Eric was the full meal deal.

Over the long term, our choices either raise us up or sink us. Like a boat that takes on water or glides effortlessly, what decisions we made, what drugs we took, who we slept with and our moral decisions all weigh on our souls to either energize us or slowly choke the sweetness from our lives. Karma tips in one direction or the other. We can either grow higher like a tree with strong roots that can withstand the storms of life, or we become weighed down with our negativity and poor decisions to the degree that we are eventually toppled. How many people have real life, love, warmth and hope in their hearts? Have many have already given up? Which will you be?

Children

Children need discipline and structure as much as they need love. When and if you have children, you set the tone, rules, goals and direction of the family, not the children. Like it or not, you are the leader, they follow. When they leave the nest, they can lead. Do not pick battles with children. You are the parent. They are the children. The tail does not wag the dog. Every issue is important. Rationalizing with a child is a waste of time. Though they can contribute, kids cannot be relied upon to choose the right answers by osmosis. They need to be told and shown the difference between right and wrong. You teach and demonstrate morality and discipline to them. They are not your friends. Adults are your friends, not your children. Do not burden your children with emotional and physical responsibilities they are not equipped to handle. They are not your counselors or confidants. Children deserve to grow up without being loaded down by their parents' problems.

Your children will watch every single thing you do to see if you follow the rules and standards you set. You cannot expect positive behavior from a child who watches a parent model something different. If you want to build your children's self esteem, stretch their comfort level. Don't protect them from every trial they encounter. Don't spoil them. Make them earn their rewards. It is the best preparation for life you can give them. Ask a lot from your kids from the time they are little. They will rise to your expectations. The world doesn't give a damn about their self-esteem. Build their self-esteem by celebrating their true achievements; not by giving empty praise that they will come to know is untrue.

"Quality time" is a myth. You will enjoy your kids most in life's simple and unscripted moments. Kids are not wind-up dolls. They cannot paint smiles on their faces on demand any better than you can. Listen to them. Be patient. Never swear at them or call them names. Be fair. Be consistent. Be positive. Most of all, let love guide everything you do to and with them. Aside from physical and sexual abuse, one of the worst things parents do is get angry and while angry and thoughtless label their kids as "stupid" or "worthless" or make much more damaging and cruel statements. These tags stay with children. Step outside until you can come back and be a compassionate and rational adult in the presence of your child. Apologize to them when you are wrong. It builds respect. Your children expect honesty and love from you, not perfection.

Be prepared to let your kids go when the time comes. Just like you wish to be liberated, so will they. Do your best, say your prayers and then set them free, like doves released.

Rapid Fire Nuggets:

Keep an ongoing "to do" list.

Have a passport you can be proud of.

Turn your cell phone off. The fate of the free world, your love life and all things in between do not hinge on whether you respond to every incoming text, Tweet, e-mail or call. Eliminate distractions. Be fully present and focused wherever you are and whomever you are with.

Read the directions first.

Do not hit the send button until you are sure who is on the CC list. Your father once broadcast a flirtatious and revealing e-mail (intended for one woman) to his entire address book. Asking people to delete it in a hastily sent second message was an open invitation for the world to examine a very limited dating rap.

Always get three medical or dental opinions. Make sure you need the procedure before you let some yahoo drill on your teeth or remove your ovaries, sage advice from your pop. Take care of your knees, ankles, hips and all of your parts. You will need them.

When all is said and done, a lot more is said than done. Surround yourself with eagles, not turkeys.

Take personal responsibility in everything you do, there are no off days.

Apologize when you are wrong. Make amends quickly.

Forgive and judge not, lest you be judged and unforgiving. Take off the millstones of judgment you wear around your neck and dance away.

Read before you default to watching movies.

Take the lowest place at the table, and let others ask you to take a better seat.

Learn something from everyone you meet. The most hopeless beggar has something to teach you, listen.

Eat what is put before you in a poor country. Even if its monkey brains, it's likely better than what the locals have. Only but for the grace of God are you not in their shoes (or crippled, or deaf, or without speech). Be humble and grateful with and for your gifts.

Never lose your sense of humor, even when the battle is going poorly. And never, but never, give up or give in to defeat. We are beaten only when we quit and when we die. Otherwise, life is all to play for, all the time. Woody Allen said, "80 percent of success is showing up." (qtd. in Keyes 161) It is true. For those who do not succeed, most often it's because they don't try, or give up at the first hurdle. Be the tortoise, not the hare.

You have time to do anything you choose to do.

When you open the refrigerator door at 11 p.m., look down at your waistline first. Then decide if you really need that bowl of ice cream or chicken wing.

Eliminate clutter from your life. If you have not used it, worn it, looked at it or forgot you had it in the last six months, give it away. Liberate yourself from that which only weighs you down.

Listen to Deep Purple turned up to ear splitting volumes in nasty airplane turbulence. A little "Highway Star" (Deep Purple, "Machine Head", 1972) is fabulous for instant courage. "Smoke on the Water" from the same album will also work in a pinch.

Final Thoughts

If you won't change the world for the better, who will? To whom does this responsibility lie? What are you waiting for? You are the future of the world. I will soon pass away and we will meet again on the other side. What becomes of this world, in direct measure, is the result of the collective decisions that you, others and I will make. What kind of world do you want? What will you create? How will you be different?

The higher you aim and the smarter and harder you work, and the higher you will fly. If you do not reach for greatness and to fulfill your Godly inspired purpose, you won't. If you do not try, what then is the meaning of your life? Why then are you here on earth? Are you just a mass of cells randomly pinging around the universe? I would suggest to you that like a salmon swimming upstream with the sole purpose of getting home, you have a goal, unique to you alone that God brought you to this earth to fulfill. While you might not know now or even for many years exactly what that is, doing your best in all things will give you the best chance to satisfy your soul, finish the mission and touch the divine.

Enough, now just go do it and get stuck in!

Your Dad loves you both very much. Know that I am very proud of you, very much in your corner and always keep you in my prayers, best wishes and thoughts. Out of all the women and little girls in the world, I am immensely grateful and proud to call you my daughters. Amen. *La Fine* (Italian for "the end").

Part 3

Marriage: "Come to Heal"

Chapter 1

"Marry her when…"

"To fear love is to fear life, and those who fear life are already three parts dead." (Russell)

Bertrand Arthur William Russell (1872 - 1970) (Irvine)

"Her" could of course be "Him."

My second trip to Nepal included volunteer work in Namche Bazaar (11,300 feet) in the Solo Khumbu region of the country where Mt. Everest is located. I had done an endodontic lecture the year before in Kathmandu and was to return several times again speaking and volunteering. Namche is the administrative center of the Solo Khumbu and is on the trekking route from the airstrip at Lukla (at 9,000 feet) where tourists often begin their journeys to Mt. Everest base camp and beyond.

After landing at Lukla, two Sherpas carried my suitcases brimming with donated dental supplies up the trail to Namche. After spending several days treating patients in the local donated dental clinic at Namche, I continued on toward the mountain. The trek from Lukla to Mt. Everest Base camp (17,000 ft) takes approximately six to eight days, depending on how acclimatized the hiker is to the altitude. After Namche, the trail passes through the famous Buddhist monastery at Tengboche (12, 700 feet) and continues to ascend. Except for one view of Ama Dablam en route to my final destination at Kala Patar (a vista from which to see Mt. Everest up close above base camp), bad weather shrouded the mountains in fog throughout the trek. The day I reached Kala Patar, the sun burst out, displaying the majesty of Chomolungma (the Mother Goddess of the World as it is known to the Nepalese in Tibetan), coincident to my acceptance of the breakup I mourned in the story that follows.

Years ago, I spent the night in a research station associated with the Italian National Research Council called EV-K2-CNR (approx 16,568 feet) in Loubche, Nepal, near the base camp of Mt. Everest's south side. (About

Marriage: "Come to Heal"

EV-K2-CNR) I was trekking by myself in the aftermath of a then recent and devastating breakup. I initiated the dissolution, but it had occurred despite my best efforts to make the relationship work. Exhausted from the trek and altitude, I could not sleep. Feeling, and being, truly alone for the first time in my life, I sobbed uncontrollably. Inconsolable, half way around the world, separated from my kids and endodontic practice, I was at the lowest ebb of my life. At that moment, I could have walked off the face of the earth and withdrawn from a successful professional life to the isolation of a remote island.

My internal conversation screamed that I did not deserve the brutal end to what had been a turbulent relationship. I asked myself repeatedly through my streaming tears "Why does this keep happening to me?" "Why can't I get it right?" "Why am I not lovable?" "Do I carry a scar that makes me defective?" A tearful boy with a clenched fist welled up inside me. He and I were one in that moment. This boy raged at every injustice ever inflicted upon him. But there was no revelation forthcoming, no comfort. A disconsolate child, I cried myself to sleep.

The next day I reached Kala Patar (approx 18,200 feet) above Mt. Everest base camp. It was as high as I have been in altitude. Little did I know that later in life I would scuba dive and come to enjoy going deep below the earth's surface on mixed gases. The sun shone brightly. A cloudless sky served as a heavenly backdrop to Mt. Everest, Lhotse and Nuptse.[51] My drive to press on was largely down to Alana and Bianca. They were all I had. I could never abandon the girls. Not knowing the future before me, but knowing why I must go home, I turned around, walked off the mountain and headed back to America.

With tincture of time, I realized my tears were misplaced. I deserved my fate. The fault did not lie with the woman involved. It was mine. I had made the errors in judgment that led to my sorrow. I had jumped into every aspect of our relationship too fast. I did not have the maturity to understand why things went wrong. When I stopped blaming and took responsibility, my worldview changed. That was the beginning of better times. My temporary scorching was a powerful lesson. I forgave myself. Forgiveness allowed me to go forward in peace. I am stronger now knowing that I can learn. I am also more humble because I know that I have much more to learn.

Among many things, I learned that "Love at first sight," (which this had been) while delicious, is not the basis for a sustainable relationship or marriage. Mr. or Mrs. Wonderful may be all that, but then again, usually not. Deciding after six weeks that you have met the love of your life (as

I had thought) is, at best, a crapshoot. If we cannot trust our feelings and judgment in the heat of the moment, how does one know when they are ready to get married?

"Come to Heal"

Marry her when you both will "Come to Heal" for the other. In a marital context, "Come to Heal" means that one person can tell the other that a behavior must change, and the other accepts it as the expression of love that it is and then makes the needed change. "Come to Heal" demonstrates an absolute commitment of each partner to the other. It represents the acceptance of both individuals that they are surrendered to the other. In essence, the relationship always comes first.

"Come to Heal" should be invoked only when an issue emerges that fatally threatens the marriage. Every divorce has a story. Alternatively, "Success leaves clues." (Butler-Bowdon 3) Whether the relationship propels connection or division depends, in large measure, on the ability to resolve differences constructively. "Come to Heal" provides a means to solve intractable problems. If one partner is causing irreparable harm and all attempts at resolution have failed, this approach can bring deeper connection or clearly tell the partners that they should go their separate ways.

Why dance around problems that threaten to sink our marriages or diminish our mutual happiness? Why speak with filters? We spend far too much of our lives tip toeing around the truth with our spouses. We take long and painful detours to avoid telling them what we really think and feel. We already know the truth about each other. We show them what is in our hearts and thoughts in a multitude of spoken and unspoken ways every single day. For example, why avoid telling your husband that being a chronic workaholic and absent husband and father must stop? If our spouse is eating himself or herself into an early grave, is it more kind to watch them commit slow suicide or speak up and try to help them look after themselves? If our spouse's behavior doesn't change after a "Come to Heal" conversation, what stronger sign is needed that we are in the wrong place, at the wrong time and with the wrong person?

A real life scenario that may require a "Come to Heal" intervention is the ex-lover that is still in contact with your beloved. Leaving unhealthy jealousy aside, what if you are uncomfortable with the relationship between your spouse and their ex (or a co-worker)? Your spouse may still have meals or drinks with this person. You may be told, if at all, after the fact about these meetings. E-mails and text messages are exchanged at all hours and justified because the person is "going through a hard time and needs a friend" or with some other rationalization. This third party is often an emotional confidante, aware of the intimate conversations occurring in your home. An emotional affair is afoot, even if not overtly physical. Any version of this situation is a toxic cocktail. It drains the couple's bank account of trust. This scenario begs for resolution with a quiet word and, if necessary, as a last resort, a "Come to Heal" conversation.

If the party engaged in the emotional affair will not stop after a "Come to Heal" conversation, they are clearly attached to the damaging behavior. How could it be otherwise? A couple's intimacy is primary. A marriage should be a place where your deepest feelings, beliefs and secrets are safe. Your relationship is just yours together and that is what makes it so special. Of all the women in the world, a man chooses a certain one to be his wife and she chooses him to be her husband, "The One." While there may be exceptions, hanging on to all who came before only suffocates the future. Speaking the truth is empowering. Tell your partner or spouse exactly what you need, what you will and will not tolerate, and do so in no uncertain terms. If they will not listen, will not change, do not care, this is a prima facie reason to leave the relationship. Conversely, if they do, the foundation of the relationship is strengthened. Progress is possible.

Many couples could use a "Come to Heal" conversation about money. Money issues, if not handled properly, are obviously a significant marital stress. If money is not flowing in abundance, how sexy is it to talk about need, limitations and what we must go without? I suspect that even famously rich celebrities privately worry whether their spouses are with them for the money instead of their unique human qualities. Money speaks to what we value as people. While money itself is neither good nor bad, what we will do to get it, or how we will spend it, says much about us. In a marriage, how our spouse treats money, how they treat us in relation to money and how they share with us says far more than anything they could articulate in words. This is not rocket science. If one partner is spending 105 percent of 100 percent of the family income, the marital financial equation is out of balance. Conflict invariably results.

In some marriages, there is often a financial passenger while the other partner is off slaying the dragon to keep the household afloat. Some people are natural pleasers. They do not like to disappoint. It strokes their pride to be the financial engine of the marriage. They cannot admit defeat. They do not wish to say to their spouse, "No, we can't afford that." Often there is an unspoken expectation that one partner is going to provide perks and rocking good times that will roll on "until death do us part."

I have known married male "artists" who would not get a job, even in the most perilous financial circumstances. Their wives were out working their butts off to allow the budding Hemingway of a husband to pontificate in coffee shops writing books that would never be finished. I've known women with significant professional training who, despite agreements to the contrary before marriage, then insist on getting pregnant, quit their careers, and subsequently expect their husbands to fund the household alone. In either relationship, it is difficult to envision that the working spouse will not become resentful unless each couple was equally supportive of the plan without coercion. When it becomes clear that Hemingway is never going to sell a story (or that he is more Milli Vanilli than Bono) he needs to get out of the coffee shop, into the want ads and do the hard work that makes a partnership.

Why do we avoid taking a stand and try to forestall the inevitable? Are we afraid of confrontation? Are we afraid of hurting the other person's feelings? Are we so enamored with our present life that we are willing to live with a jagged rock in our shoe whose pain is somehow overcome by the security of the present relationship? Many years ago, Fram oil filters had advertisements where a car mechanic tells the viewer, "You can pay me now (buy a new oil filter), or pay me later (to rebuild the engine)." Whether in oil filters or marital dilemmas, the later fix is always more expensive.

How often have we waited patiently hoping for change only to find out later that our spouse cared more for their selfish interests than our relationship? We can dance around a truth for years hoping for miraculous change before acknowledging that our spouse was committed to something, anything, more than they were to us. While a sad truth, it is one we should admit when present. Barriers to intimacy, among many, include: selfishness, addiction in many forms, unwillingness to protect a spouse (especially from a toxic in-law or third party), untreated depression, insecurity, jealousy, lack of forgiveness and respect and emotional affairs in addition to overtly sexual ones. Each of these issues is a torpedo aimed directly at the love that hopefully was the genesis of the marriage. If unchecked, they will sink the couple.

When we speak about these concerns with our spouses in a "Come to Heal" conversation, they may deflect our desire for positive change.

They may have reasons why their behavior should continue. They may get defensive and answer questions with questions. Given enough time, in some cases, it will become patently clear that they have no intention of cooperating or change. Left unchecked, out of our good intentions and misguided love, we can easily become an accessory to a crime committed against our marriage and enable our partners to abuse us. Who wants to be in such a relationship where the ground shifts, where everything is negotiable, where neither party is really sure what they do or do not have? This iteration of marriage is instability personified.

When it becomes clear that your spouse is not going to change, especially given time after a loving "Come to Heal" conversation, leave. Leave or face the bleak prospect of surrendering your happiness for an indefinite period of time and coming away physically, mentally and financially spent. In the endodontic world, there is wisdom based on the German proverb that says, "Better an end with horror than horror without end." (Lukacs 319) Sometimes the tooth needs to be removed after things have gone wrong and no amount of skill can save it. While immensely painful, facing up to the repulsive facts, especially when we know we must leave, is the first step toward healing.

Dark Rooms, Agreed Upon Faith, Walking the Talk

Marry her when there are no ghosts and no subject between you is off limits. Your martial house should not contain dark rooms whose doors have never been opened.[52] Lift the curtains, let in the light. Marry the warts, scars and flesh wounds as well as the innumerable bright spots. Marry her when she can look through every file on your computer, every message on your e-mail program, every number on your cell phone. There should be no private world except the one that you share privately with her. If you want intimacy, give it to her first.

Marry her when you have an agreed upon faith, even if that faith is true atheism. In essence, agree on what you believe and what fundamental principles guide your relationship. Anything else is a ship without a rudder that will predictably run aground. While people can spout all kinds of spiritual gobbledygook, at some level, some things are OK and some things are not OK in any marriage, irrespective of the presence or absence of faith. For two people in the trenches, living together, trudging off to work and raising kids, some code of morality and ethics must be present and roughly equivalent and agreed-upon by both parties. In Biblical terms, the couple must be equally yoked. (Corinthians 16.4) While there are exceptions,

89

couples of widely divergent spiritual beliefs and life philosophies are more likely to hit the martial rocks head on. Spiritual and religious beliefs guide actions. Decisions on whether the family eats pork, allows their children to play with plastic guns (or have real ones), drinks alcohol, uses 2 percent milk or soy, smokes, drinks coffee, uses animal products, gambles, spanks their children or allows young children to sleep with the couple all require agreement. These foundational decisions, among many others, must be made irrespective of whether the couple goes to the same religious service or none at all. A relative balance in beliefs positively predicts a couple's compatibility. Ignoring this truth is perilous. A belief that because "I love her, she loves me, and we'll find a way" is a prescription to not only run your martial ship aground, but to do so at full speed ahead, hatches open and loaded with live munitions.

Marry her when you both have proven that you will keep your word when the other is not looking. If a man cheats at board games or his taxes, he will cheat on his wife when her back is turned. Trust does not come easily or cheaply. Trust arises out of proven experience. Over time, one's integrity emerges. Trust cannot be bought; it cannot be fast-forwarded by dating services or Internet matching sites. While you might meet someone through these means, this does not short circuit the time needed to develop trust. Much like the roots of a tree gaining stability to support the trunk, tincture of time will make all the ingredients (soil, water, nutrients) have a chance to work together. It takes time to see if the talk gets walked.

For most couples, the truth, intimacy and communication needed to make a marriage work predictably will take at least two years of dating. While there may be exceptions, it will usually not happen in two days, two weeks or two months. Two years is enough time for old flames to re-emerge, high school reunions, funerals, births, anniversaries, Christmas parties, Bar Mitzvahs, visits by the crazy uncle, job changes, delayed flights, lottery jackpots and other abundant good fortune. Two years is enough time to experience real life, not the orgasmic fantasy world that characterizes the beginning of many relationships. A time that often hoodwinks us into believing that our dripping infatuation will continue forever. Over a two-year period, we can see how our intended partner handles a variety of everyday events that will be our life together. Future landmines and strengths can be read like a book if only we will take off our rose-colored glasses. Two years tells us whether the seeds of a deeper relationship can take root. We must be patient. Only ample time will let us know what we are grabbing a hold of by its consummation in marriage. It will also tell us what we must let go of to make it work. A two-year time frame allows us to decide based on hard cold experience rather than hope that our intended is the right person for us.

The Business Side of Marriage, Time and Forgiveness

Marriage has a "business" side. Conducting the business of marriage adroitly is an essential underpinning to a deepening emotional and sexual connection. Checks have to be written, taxes paid, the plumber called. It is in these things that some couples lose altitude and ultimately crash. If we can't trust our spouses to send the check when promised, how can we trust them with our innermost hopes, fears and needs? If a mother has been doing everything for her boy that he should have done for himself since he was born, when he marries, who will be doing the heavy lifting on the business side of his marriage? My bet is his wife.

Marry her when there is no rush to do so. One party should never pressure another into marriage. Because a biologic clock ticks or a man believes he is ready to get married, are not reasons to either marry or have children. Temporal decisions tend to be poor ones. If the decision to marry is rushed, the certainty of the decision is rarely as strong. If the other person is leaning on you to marry and you are not ready, simply say "No." Tell them to wait or to leave. Acquiescing to make them happy when you are unsure breeds resentment.

"Its about time that I married, I am in my 30s now (or 40s, or late 20s)" is a tepid rationale for marriage. These speak of a void that the other person must fill. It makes the other the solution to our needs and wants. This is a heavy, if not impossible, burden for anyone to carry. Believing that our significant other represents "my best last chance at love" or "a love that won't come my way again" is thinly masked desperation. We should be searching for the right mate, first, last and always, never to fill a short-term void.

Love will come around as many times as we are willing to let it, forever. God did not put us on this earth to be lonely. We are most often our own worst enemies at holding off love. Love is always there when we are ready for it. Holding onto past hurts is wholly unproductive. The more razor wire we throw up, the harder it is for love to reach us. We are all lovable. We are all desirable. We all deserve love. When we tear down our walls through forgiveness, love will flood us in tsunami proportions. We must forgive ourselves. We must forgive those who have wronged us.

Love and fear are mutually incompatible. Love is not conditional. Love is present or isn't, it has no shade of gray.

Holding in bitterness and withholding forgiveness are chains I will not wear. What made my love with my wife, Laura, possible is simple: I accepted that I had made mistakes and hurt others in the past. I do not wish that to be my future. It is not my future. I wish to live passionately each day as fulfilled as possible. I cannot do that being angry with my parents. I cannot do that carrying around an axe to grind at every injustice committed against me in past relationships and in business. I take personal responsibility for my mistakes. I have sought to make amends where possible and avoid repetition. Any other option is to live with the pain of divorce, isolation, and a simmering anger at every past and future slight no matter how small. That is not a prescription for happiness.

All the counseling in the world will not succeed unless we come to grips with a simple and painful gravitational fact. If we are honest with ourselves, we will see that we own a big part of our failures. We participated in the relationship whose pain may linger in our hearts. We exercised poor judgment when wisdom and love required a different action from us. We must forgive ourselves and forgive those around us for this past. Once we take responsibility for our actions and make amends for our mistakes, we can move forward, toward love.

And finally, marry her when you know that when she is old, wrinkly and shows a bit more gravitational pull, that you only want her hand in yours on the porch swing. Then and only then is it time to make the commitment. Taking these steps will, to a high degree of certainty, keep you from ever having to ask the question found in the fifth chapter, part three of *Dead Stuck*, "Should I stay or should I go?" (The Clash, Combat Rock, 1982) That is a cool rock song by The Clash, it should not be a tough relationship decision.

Chapter 2

Finding "The One"

"Such is the common process of marriage. A youth and maiden exchange meeting by chance, or brought together by artifice, exchange glances, reciprocate civilities, go home, and dream of one another. Having little to divert attention, or diversify thought, they find themselves uneasy when they are apart, and there conclude that they shall be happy together. They marry, and discover what nothing but voluntary blindness had before concealed; they wear out life in altercations, and charge nature with cruelty." (Johnson, Rasselas 69)

Samuel Johnson (1709 – 1784) (Johnson)

I have grown to learn the importance of listening well. Listening well earns trust. Over time, I have become a keen listener to my patients. In the office, most patients are afraid that their concerns will not be heard. They also fear that even if they speak up, that, beneath the words, they will not be understood. I have found this to be true not only in clinical endodontic practice, but in finding a mate as well. As I have listened with intention, my satisfaction in both my career and marriage has improved dramatically.

I am a hopeless romantic. I am also pragmatic as hell. I do not like the term "soul mate." It is froufrou. Relationships work or do not work on the basics, not whether two souls are somehow synched to an ethereal rhythm. Fundamental questions like "Does my spouse listen to me?" or "Can we resolve our differences productively?" are strong predictors of a relationship's success. This has nothing to do with seeing auras, past life regression, raw sexual attraction or the all-encompassing term "chemistry." We need a spouse who, when confronted with a potential conflict, will stop dead in their tracks, sit down, look us in the eye, put their feet flat on the floor, and say "Honey, I hear you. I can see that you are upset (frustrated, hurt, whatever). How can I help?" Or, when hearing good news, will say, "Honey, I can see you are excited, tell me more." Such effective communication can help avoid the hidden crevasses and poised avalanches present that we often choose to ignore. The desire for connection, both verbal and non-verbal, is one means to identify the person who clearly values our relationship more than their past hurts, present whims and immediate need. These clues will help identify "The One."

The tone of conversation above, in one fashion or another, is a prerequisite for achieving intimacy. Through such conversations while dating, we can decide over time whether we have a match with "The One" to whom we are contemplating marriage. Healthy couples communicate this way. It happens because they want it to. They are committed to one another. We can all communicate with this intention if we choose by being present and focusing our attention fully on our intended or actual spouses. Alternatively, miscommunication arises when one partner simply does not care enough to listen and respond in a way that brings connection. Rather, they are selfishly focused on being right and unfortunately they often hurt the other person in return for some past slight, real or imagined.

Early relationships are both intoxicating and frightening. When we are in one, we cannot dictate or know the true intentions and nature of the other person without experience and time. Coincident to this reality, a new and significant relationship takes us on a path to an unknown destination. Consciously or unconsciously, to protect themselves, there are those who sabotage prospective relationships in their infancy. It may be easier to hold off love than to face the risk and hurt that may come from reaching out for love and failing. Treating relationships like a game, these individuals choose isolation. For them, loneliness is the known evil, the known pain. Fearing a lack of control, even if a loving connection means a far more enriching life experience, they chose to accept a less satisfying relationship than what they desire.

Such fear, false pride and a lack of self-esteem can lead to serial temporary relationships. Similar to a diet of fast food, these liaisons fill a void but ultimately are unsatisfactory because they are incomplete. Such "drive by" relationships never reveal our weakest spots to others. In essence we are not known completely to one another. In exchange, we do not know nor do we love the other in their entirety. I believe human beings seek real and deepening relationships within which they are completely vulnerable to one another. Overcoming fear of intimacy is a choice. It requires patience, time and common sense. I do not believe that loving and being loved, with communication as one piece of this exchange, requires training. We have the innate capabilities for love. It is only a matter of caring enough to do so. We care enough to give and receive love, or we don't. Love is ultimately a very simple exchange. Do we need a "to do" list to tell our spouse we love them before we go to sleep and kiss them? Do we need to be reminded, as if it was a skill to be learned, that we should ask what we could get for dinner if we are at the store and the meal is not yet planned? If asked to play golf on Saturday and we are unsure of our spouse's plans, can we not simply call and find out before agreeing? If we are displeased with our spouse for some reason, can we not speak to them with love and civility rather than scorn and accusation? All the books, retreats, television shows, advice and tapes cannot replace what is a simple desire, to seek greater intimacy because we care. If we have any doubts, the simplest way to find out is to ask them! Start with, "Honey, what do you need? I love you."

Finding "The One"

Finding a spouse is not a complicated proposition; we only make it complicated by imposing wholly arbitrary time frames onto something that just cannot be forced. For those who want to be married, and yet have no prospects, my advice is simple. Wait patiently, it will happen.

Men, you might be at the international foods section of your local supermarket buying spotted dick the holiday pudding and turn around to find a face smiling at you, wondering what you are doing with a spotted dick in your hand. Spotted dick was once good enough for Jerry Hall as means for getting her suitors to prove themselves. (Greenberg) It might just work for you!

Women, being genuine is attractive to men. When you are in the supermarket watching that cute guy holding his spotted dick, you don't need a pickup line. You don't need to be amazing. You don't need to say anything profound. You don't need to show any leg or have dazzling clothes. Maybe just start with "Hello." Or, if you must say something pithy, try a winner like "How's that spotted dick working out for you?" If the boy has any game, he might just laugh and reply "At the moment, quite well. May I buy you a cup of coffee?" When people ask how you met, now you really have a story. Perhaps it is even simpler. Just be kind to people. A potential spouse will gravitate toward you, in part, because of your gentleness. This, combined with finding your purpose in life, is all the mojo you will ever need.

How patient have you been in trying to find "The One"? Relationships are not like getting a coffee at Starbucks, a place where we are provided with instant comfort. We cannot walk into a store and leave with a warm fuzzy connection as delicious as a white chocolate mocha. Relationships are work. Marriage is the hardest work of all. It is not easy now, never has been, never will be. Marriage and discovering if your intended spouse is "The One" takes time. There is risk. Risk that you will get your heart ripped out, stomped on and thrown back at you shredded. Wisdom entails knowing to whom we should give our heart. Wisdom dictates we must be extremely careful in making the choice of to whom we give ourselves over at the deepest level. Sex is easy, deeper love is much harder. Like water flowing downhill, how often have we blindly gone down the easy path of slipping into bed with an intriguing date to find out later, for a variety of reasons ranging from disease, pregnancy and infidelity that, this temporary roll in the hay was a bad idea and ultimately hurt everyone around us? Did we exercise any common sense before we dropped our trousers or lifted our skirts?

Patience takes character. We live in a world that screams to us in advertising, music and movies that a piece of latex is all that is required to make sexual decisions and that there is no moral consequence to our sexuality. If we were aliens asked to observe and comment on the popular culture, the permutations of who has, does, could, would, might or should exchange genetic material with whom is beyond comprehension. From an alien point of view, we be bunnies, off like honeymoon pajamas to the next soirée.

I find this whole suggestion tragic, albeit pervasive in our culture. It presupposes that we are robots without feelings. If there is no right and wrong and we can have sex without consequence or commitment, the experience carries with it no long-term significance to our psyches, self-esteem and emotional health. I am not at all convinced of this proposition. How many Lotharios hold their grandchildren later in life in a functional and loving family setting? How many women have had dozens of partners to one day find that they are now in a happy, committed long-term relationship that is secure and growing in depth? I know the euphemisms of "its just sex," "consenting adults," "friends with benefits," "f!*& bunnies" and other such repartee. Does any of this really take us to a committed long-term monogamous relationship? Does this strategy provide us a safe place where, out of everyone else on the planet, our spouse values us as "The One"? Thinking rationally before acting will go a long way toward making a solid first step in building relationships founded on trust. Besides, as a man, if your date tells you she has bonked every guy in town, including some of the married ones, aside from sexually transmitted disease concerns, how can you trust that she means what she says or that she will remain faithful? As a man, what if you have jumped with reckless abandon into as many rodeos as possible and kept the pictures and movies to prove it? How can she trust you? Will you be faithful to her? How many ghosts, fears and insecurities do we want to sleep with? How snake bitten can we begin and still end up happy?

All of this, in large measure, begs the question, that of knowing how to find "The One." We must work on ourselves first to make sure that we bring to the table the qualities we want from others. Do we have something unique other than our physical appearance and our money that makes us singularly desirable? What is special and appealing about us? Why should someone forsake all others for us? Have we vanquished our own demons? Have we learned from our mistakes? Are we passionately pursuing our true purpose on this planet? Are we fully ready to commit to the other person on every level? What game do we have that makes us appealing beyond the ordinary everyday?

What is the last book we read that gave us something new to talk about, a book on a subject we knew relatively little about? What have we done to expand our horizons? When was the last time we tried something foreign to us? Cooked a new recipe, baked bread, brewed beer, learned how to filet a salmon? In essence, as men, what are we doing that would make a woman say, "Wow, that boy is the cat's meow. That's a tiger I'd like to be introduced to." How often are we on a date and despite having a throbbing physical attraction, all we can talk about are our past relationships and what movies we last saw? If that is all we have, we do not have the basis for a marriage. He or she is not "The One."

Ideally, you and your intended should be coming to the relationship healed. Talking about your ex spouse (and especially disparaging them), no matter how problematic that person might have been, is a clear sign that you are not ready for marriage. Your new spouse deserves the best of you. You deserve the best of them. You exist to create a safe home, a new life together. You do not exist to live in an unhappy past. While marriage can help complete you, it cannot, in and of itself, heal your past relationship wounds. The far greater likelihood is that you will repeat the same patterns and mistakes. Come to your new marriage starting fresh. It is an impossible burden to ask another to make you healed and whole. No matter how hard they try, your spouse cannot fix you; you must do it for yourself. The best anyone can do is to take you as you are, not as anyone hopes you will be in some perfect future, a future that does not now nor will likely ever exist.

We must be honest with ourselves and, just as importantly, with others. If we know we will never marry or change something they wish changed, we must tell prospective lovers. If we love something, anything, so much that it will always stand in the way of a married relationship, we must let this be openly known. It is better to say "I do not know" when we do not know what we really want than to promise something we are not sure we can deliver. We should not use others for our temporary amusement or to selfishly fill our needs for sex or companionship. We should not lead another on that a relationship is going somewhere when we know it is not. If we will never leave Tillamook, Oregon, because to us it is the epicenter of all that is good in the universe, fair enough. However, we must be truthful if our lover lives in Enid, Oklahoma and expects that one day Tillamook is moving to Enid. If Tillamook is never moving to Enid, Enid needs to know as soon as possible. It is cruel to pretend otherwise.

Lapses in truth cause real damage. They stay with us. They raise the bar for the one deceived to trust again when asked to believe the next person who makes similar promises. We rarely see the wreckage in our rear view mirrors when we drive away to our new "soul mate" because "All is fair in love and war."(George Latimer Apperson 355) How many single mothers have trusted a man only to find out that "I love you" meant "I just want you for tonight"? How many children are without fathers because such a sperm donor decided that their pleasure was more important than taking responsibility for their actions? Integrity matters, all the time.

How many conquests and kills out "hunting" does a man need before he is a "man" or "wins" or reaches some perceived milestone of stamina? Other than to feed his ego, what does this really serve? Why does it have to be the woman's responsibility to "protect" herself? Where is the man behaving as honorably as he would hope his father, mother, sons, daughters and wife once did or does now? If each and every one of us were to answer these questions within the true values of our own conscience, values that ideally should be centered on "Do unto others..." (Luke 6:31) collectively, we would inflict less harm on each other. Actions centered on such a value would be a positive development in our present world. Sexual compatibility is hugely important. That said, if men spent as much time considering the comprehensive proposition marriage entails rationally with their big heads, their employment of the little head would be far more satisfactory.

Marriage: "Come to Heal"

The male critic will cry foul, "You want me to be faithful to one woman? You're nuts, everyone cheats! Don't even think of telling me what to do or try to limit me in any way." Some do cheat, but are they happy? Where does their "hunting" lead them in the end? How many men scamming trim are cheered at visualizing their wives and girlfriends having Kung Fu sex with the pool boy? The double standard is grossly insulting to the women in our lives. Women should be honored respectfully as our queens, because they are "The One" and nothing less.

How then does one date and get to know the other person without jumping into bed quickly, moving in and making this newfound object of affection the ready made answer to our problems, the final piece of the puzzle, our "everything"? How do we know we want to buy the car if we do not take it for a very long test drive? Every couple has their own means of coming to know if the other is "The One", but a foolproof litmus test is consistent honesty over a two-year period. He said he would call at 11:30 p.m. when he got into the hotel in Mandan, he did. He said he would pick the kids up at 5 p.m., he did. He said that he would make dinner Saturday night and do the dishes, he did. He said he would deposit the money, he did. "She" could be substituted for "He" in any of these statements. Each of these steps is a path to trust, a path that will often take about two years to walk to know if we have found "The One." Easy peasy.

It is vital we get this right. Try as we may, we cannot negotiate the rules of marriage after the game has begun. There are no dress rehearsals even if we jokingly refer to a first wife as "the starter" or a second spouse as a "do over." Whoever the first wife was, the deep hurt inflicted was mutual. Best to get it right the first time. Divorce is the nuclear option. It leaves a very big hole, is radioactive and forever changes everyone who lives in the neighborhood. Divorce, especially in America, is an immensely destructive sport where the winner is the last person standing. Its popularity as an escape option reinforces a cynical belief that marriage is an outmoded institution, an institution in which we try to squeeze out as many good years as we can get before we run into the arms of our next "sweetheart." Divorce reinforces the cynical belief that once a poorly conceived marriage goes stale, it is time to pack up our toys and move down the road to greener pastures, larger breasts and tighter thighs only to fatten the calf of the divorce attorneys.

Sandra Tsing Loh, in an article for The Atlantic magazine, asks, "Why do we still insist on marriage? Sure, it made sense to agrarian families before 1900, when to farm the land, one needed two spouses, grandparents, and a raft of children. But now that we have white-collar work and washing machines, and our life expectancy has shot from 47 to 77, isn't the idea of lifelong marriage obsolete?" (Loh) Sandra, people insist on marriage because they want to be truly known and still be loved intimately by another without barriers despite their flaws. They want to give back the same love and acceptance. What you miss is that divorce, most often, is the result of a poor initial choice and a lack of planning. The fault lies not with the institution of marriage.

Understandably, humans do not like to give over their power. Many successful professional people are challenged in marriage because the skills that destroy the competition in commerce are catastrophically bad for couples. These people are used to giving orders. Such assertiveness leads to relationship obliteration. Our spouses are not our chattel. Relationships work because the couple decides that their mutual association is more beneficial and nurturing than their walking apart in this life. At its best, two people submit all they have and all they will be in the future to one another. They are "in." They are "all in, unconditionally, all the time" Life is tough enough without compromising away from this ideal. Any step back from this level of commitment is like a cake that does not have the right measurements or ingredients. Such a cake neither looks nor tastes right. There would be far less divorce if such a level of commitment and seriousness were accorded the choice of whom we marry.

If we want all there is from marriage, we cannot hold back. We cannot stand at the altar saying, "Yes" with our lips and yet have our fingers crossed behind our backs. We cannot later state that we meant "I love you" when we said it but that now we take it back. Do not say, "I love you" and "for better and for worse and in sickness and in health" unless you are unconditionally committed. Do not say it unless you mean it. Do not go there until it is real. Have the integrity to be patient. It will happen. When you are truly ready, you will meet "The One." One who will love you enough to wipe up your vomit after your chemotherapy, someone who will feed you when you can't help yourself, in essence, someone who meant every word on their wedding day. Find someone who will "Come to Heal" with you. When you have that, you have found "The One."

Chapter 3

For Men

"There is no perfect marriage, for there are no perfect men." (qtd. in Krieger 264)

Old French Proverb (Krieger 264)

For all of the political correctness that exists in America today, men and women have profound differences. My experiences with male patients and female patients have been just as divergent. Suffice it to say, dealing with male patients is usually a matter of answering three questions: Is it going to hurt? How much is it going to cost? How long will this take? These questions can be translated as: "I would not be here if I did not have to be" "If I can afford it, lets do it" and "As soon as we are done, get me the hell out of here." Men outside an endodontic office are much the same. We know what we want. We know what we do not want. The prevailing mentality is let's get this done. We want to be off slaying the dragon, whatever our dragon might be. Whether this is nature, nurture or both, I do not know. It just is. In any event, our haste can create isolation from the women we love.

Men, it's not complicated. Having the loving, sexual and vibrant marriage we want is within our grasp. Like championships that are built on executing the basics well, having a good marriage is much the same. It is the little things, the fundamentals done right, that provide the platform for success. These fundamentals are not expensive, complex or even particularly challenging to carry out.

No matter what difficulty you face with your wife, you loved her once, and if you do your part chances are she will do hers and together you will move forward. Alternatively, in the long term, if you do your part and she does not respond, it's time to leave and find a woman who will meet you halfway. Doing your part is simple. When you come home, start with something like, "Honey, how are you?" Inquire about her first. No matter what, listen to your wife. There is plenty of time for you to download about the business trip, who did what to whom, when, where, why and how. Find out how she really is. Do not start describing your day until she is done. If she listens to you first, make sure you give her not only equal time but also equal attention. Ask about her job, her business trip, what she would like to do in the upcoming weekend, the kids if she is the primary caregiver and all their recent goings-on. For this time, it is all about her, not about you.

No matter how bad you want to watch the game, go fishing with your buddies, play golf or fix the car, when your wife needs to have a chat about something she is interested in or needs to get off her chest, do it. Face her, look her in the eye, be quiet and listen. Put your feet flat on the floor. Unfold your arms. You do not need a beer, cigarette, cocktail, sandwich or other distraction to have this conversation. Turn your cell phone off. Turn the radio off. Turn the television off. Put the kids in another room. Focus on her and her alone. Listening well is a foundational earth anchor to a growing and healthy relationship.

Never try to fix her problems, never, ever. She needs you to listen, not act. Ask her questions, care about the answer. Give her suggestions only if she asks for your help. Never interrupt your wife. Never, ever say, "Yes honey, but what about…?" to refute her. Do not deflect the conversation on to some safe or tangential topic to avoid getting to the heart of the matter. Do not answer her questions with questions to avoid her. If you must ask a question, something like "What do you need from me?" "How can I help with that?" "How can we solve this together?" are productive questions. Knowing you genuinely care, she will open up to you as never before.

Having an intelligent, confident and emotionally secure spouse is an essential pillar to building your relationship. Never belittle your wife. Never worry that she might be smarter, more articulate, more cultured or ultimately better than you at something. She already is on some levels whether you want to admit it or not. My wife has bags of talent I can only dream of possessing. I want to learn from her and expand my own horizons with her.

Marriages get stronger through trials. They are tested constantly. If you do not argue with your spouse or there is no tension at some healthy level, your relationship lacks passion and may be slowly dying. Disagreements, if they are resolved well, are opportunities for deeper connection. Conflict cannot be resolved if we default to a mentality of "you are wrong and I am right," in which we stomp off to our caves to lick our wounded pride. When our wives come to us with an issue, we must accept that even though the issue may have no importance for us, it must have some significance for them. We cannot default to telling our wives that they just do not understand, or worse yet, telling them straight out that they are wrong. There is little in a life that is black and white. There is much gray, as for example, in politics. While we may hold our donkey or elephant close to our heart, many political issues can be looked at from a wide variety of perspectives. If you believe that you are the sole repository of knowledge about any issue, stasis results. Your wife may know the issue far better than you. We cannot hear our wives or understand them, if we are speaking instead of listening with open minds. Disagreement is essential to the health of the relationship, as fire is healthy for the forest. It takes away the brush to leave the strongest trees and replenishes the soil.

Marital disagreements are often power struggles. They have little to do with the issue at hand. The martial conflict that is resolved well is the one where both parties intend resolution and want a deeper connection, not to "win." Consider also that you might be wrong, that you might be arguing the point only to save face. You may be disagreeing so as not to appear vulnerable and found to be deficient. From a woman's perspective, what is essential for sex is an intimacy that is impossible without skilled conflict resolution, a component essential for a deepening love. Lovemaking without this intimacy at a heart level is disingenuous.

Jealousy is for losers. Do not marry her if you doubt her fidelity. She should not marry you if she doubts yours. Do not isolate your wife; let her be all that she was meant to be. Be glad that she has friends outside your marriage, just as you have friends too. As long as your connection is not harmed in any way, she should feel free to socialize with whomever she wishes. Your wife will come home enthusiastically to be with you. Marriage is like a very large ranch in South Dakota, a place within whose boundaries there is freedom.

Make it safe for your woman. Make her your object of desire. Would you like it if she were hoarding images of men in various states of undress? There would be more mutual desire if she knew that you do not judge her appearance. Who cares if she might be a little flatter, rounder or beanpole than you want? When was the last time you looked in the mirror? Do you look like Brad, Lance, or David in the buff? If she knows she is completely safe with you in every way and that she comes first, she will rock your world much harder than any surgically enhanced floozy ever could.

If you do not want to be faithful, don't plan on being faithful, have no desire to be faithful, then either don't marry her or tell her in advance. Do not break her heart by asking her to believe that you meant the words "forsaking all others" that was likely, or will be, in your vows. Tell her the truth, always. Be vulnerable. She is your greatest champion, best friend and biggest asset in the foxhole. She certainly once was and can be going forward. You married her to be your "closer," your "go to" player when the game is on the line. She has resources, ideas and capabilities you may not even know about. If you always have to be right and have power, how can she show you?

You may have once told her that she was "the one" or some variation of this meaning. You probably even wrote her a card or two while you we courting her to tell her so. Prove it. Since she was once all that, she certainly still is! Your relationship should be nurtured and tended like a garden. It is an ongoing and never ending work with immeasurable long-term benefits. Get your gloves on.

When she asks for something within reason, give it to her. Never withhold something that makes her world safer, more fulfilling and more loving. Elevate her. She will elevate you. If she wants to go back to school, find a way. If she wants to get a job, hire a recruiter. If she wants to take yoga, basket weaving, a cooking class, whatever, support her and go and try the class if she asks. Be open-minded; while Ashtanga technique[53] may have no appeal for you, she will love you more for the effort and you might just like it.

The little things that happen between a man and a woman make all the difference. On a daily basis, ask your wife what she needs. What can you get at the store for her? Do the laundry. Cut the grass without being asked. Empty the garbage. Do the dishes. Do the laundry. Pick up after yourself. The moldy pizza under the bed needs to go. Leave love notes under her pillow. After she gets a root canal take her out for ice cream or give her a massage. Be actively engaged in her life. Be a positive and loving force for her. Be her biggest fan, her most trusted advisor, her true safe harbor.

When you leave the house, always kiss her goodbye. When you write a note or say goodbye on the phone, tell your wife how much you love her. While highly individual, find physical touches that express your love. When you come home, go to her first and kiss her. The kids, the TV and the refrigerator can wait. If one part of her clothing or appearance sparkles, tell her, even if the rest is a bit askew. Ask about the books she is reading, why she likes them, what she is learning. You are not an island in your own home. Marriage is a living, breathing fire that we either fuel or let die. The choice is ours.

Chapter 4

For Women

"It is the plain women who know about love; the beautiful women are too busy being fascinating." (Esar 830)

Katharine Hepburn (1907 – 2003)(Corliss)

For those women I have known personally and professionally that have been less than happy with their relationships, I have observed commonality as to the origin of some aspects of their discontent. They are detailed here.

Ladies, it is not complicated. You do not need breasts so firm they touch your chin when you sneeze; you do not need the continental divide, Mt. Everest or K2[54] on your chest. You do not need your butt sucked or your private parts lifted to regain a certain tension you mistakenly think will give you some advantage in the heat of the moment. You do not need attire from Prada, Burberry, D&G, or baubles from Tiffany & Co. You do not need to be blonde. You do not need to jump into your jeans from tall heights. Your thongs, tattoos and other private details do not need to become public when you bend over for you to be awe-inspiring.

You are inherently attractive to men. Capable and strong women with bags of self-esteem and confidence are irresistibly seductive. The man that is a keeper is the one who will respect you as an equal, for what you really are, not because you have chemically smoothed your wrinkles or are showing what you believe might be the right amount of bosom to hold their attention.

The natural essence of a woman and her profound difference from man are more than enough. The rest of it just clouds the issue and, if anything, deflects energy away from core needs, loving and being loved. Just be yourself, be patient, do not fret. He is out there, and one day, if you are authentic and honest, the earth can and will move for you. Many men could and would rock your world if only you would chose wisely and then let them in. Trying to change yourself to conform to a norm that does not exist in reality and only exists in a make believe world as a slinky thinly clad anorexic bimbo on the side of a building is futility personified. Coincidently, I have seen the same bimbo displayed on buildings from Europe to Taipei. For my money, the billboard tells all the women in Taipei that they should be Caucasian, do away with their epicanthic folds and hold a hat over their breasts while naked as a jay bird. The advertising implies that any deviations from this stylized concept of women's fashion or appearance will not be attractive to a man. I can only imagine the negative self-image that arises for those not matching this perceived ideal look, shape, clothing or jewelry. How many women match this image?

A man is attracted in large measure by being wanted. A woman who desires him for both heads, the one on his shoulders and the smaller one, is a powerful force. This dynamic is wholly independent from what clothes, shoes, jewelry, makeup, pant size or hair color a women possesses. It is ironic that we often do not wear these things when we are making love. These accoutrements are wholly surplus to the requirements in the bedroom. It is probably a good idea that the pits are shaved, but beyond that 99 percent of the rest of it is all a girl thing that guys frankly do not pay much attention to.

Clothing is a means of providing function, fashion and art, not an anatomy lesson. You do not need your skirts so low that your short and curlies are on display when you serve coffee (been there, seen that). You might do these things for yourself, as a means of self-expression, fashion or body art. That is one thing; however, when you do them solely to attract men, you lose a bit of your true self and surrender to someone else's vision of what is alluring. Ultimately, all these actions make you look a lot more like everyone else, essentially a lot plainer Jane. You are telling men, and everyone around you, that you, when presented with the choice to be unique, choose to be one of the crowd. While there might be protection in numbers, from this man's perspective the attractive woman has something to say that I have not heard before. In this woman's presence I am exposed to something new in appearance, a bona fide original. How can you be genuine and fresh? That is up to you. Nevertheless, there is room for creative self-expression that does not require you to cut, color or change yourself, even if another wields the scalpel.

You do not need to silence your voice and be stupid because you do not want to threaten a man. You do not need to wear gallons of makeup, have the perfect shoes or even a matching ensemble. Whether pear- or catwalk-shaped, you do not need to change what you are, how you look, act or dress either to attract a man, or to have happiness with him.

Some of you may be changing yourselves for your girlfriends. If so, what does this really say about your friends? More importantly, what does it say about you? Has it brought you the relationships you seek with either a man or your girlfriends? Perhaps there is a better way. Just be you. You are more than enough as you are.

Chapter 5

Should I Stay or Should I Go?

"I wonder among all the tangles of this mortal coil, which one contains tighter knots to undo, and consequently suggests more tugging, and pain, and diversified elements of misery, than the marriage tie." (Wolff 221)

Edith Wharton (1862 – 1937) (Edith Wharton, 75, Is Dead in France)

My endodontic practice has helped keep me sane at times of stress in my life, relationship and otherwise. Hours slip when I am "in the zone" (treating patients). Much like an athlete where time disappears during a game, being passionate about endodontics and working with people has given me a refuge when I might otherwise have stewed in discontent. I am grateful for this.

What of a relationship that clearly needs to end but from which both parties will not move on to avoid the pain of leaving? Little thought is often given to the relief that letting go will bring. How many years of isolation and loneliness must pass before the obvious right step is taken in these desperate situations? Relationships are like rubber bands. Stretched too far, they break. They do not glue back together. If you know, in your deepest heart of hearts, that your rubber band is broken, it is time to leave. A happy and fulfilling relationship has, at its core, two people who lovingly say "yes" to each other without conditions. If such love is not powering the relationship's engine, it will not work, end of story.

Two mental audiotapes, the staying tape and the leaving tape often manifest uncertainty over the future direction of a troubled relationship. In an incessant loop, they slowly drive us crazy. We hear the leaving tape and we make a firm decision to go. Feeling convicted as to a future course of action, we know what we want. We will end the relationship. As we decide how to tell our spouse, the impact of our decision sinks in. We hear a voice that says, "Yes, but what about…" as the staying tape engages. As we definitively decide to stay and gut it out, the leaving tape begins. This unabated pattern continues indefinitely until there is such pain that we are forced to act for self-preservation or the decision is made for us. In the present, though, we are neither willing to accept the troubled relationship nor willing to pay the price to leave and start again.

In the absence of a decision, there is ambiguity in our every action. How can we plan for the future, be that next week or next year, if we do not know where we will live and with whom? Our relationship uncertainty causes us to rationalize our decisions. We make excuses. We hope that it will be different next time. We excoriate ourselves and think that we are solely responsible for our misery. We deceive ourselves to believe that trying harder and loving the other person more fully will improve the relationship. It does not.

We wish and hope for these things because once upon a time, the relationship was good. The problem is, it has not been good for a while. So long that we cannot even remember when that last was. As we reflect, the relationship has not been good since the beginning. Likely a time when we did not even know our lover well and we were both burning with desire. The flame has long since died. Left in its charred haze are decisions of consequence. In the sobering daylight of the present moment, we pay in gold bricks for the privilege of being with this person. Long after the excitement of the purchase, we awoke to the ugly facts that we have walked down the aisle, had children, bought houses, shared our toothbrushes and declared to the world that our spouse was "The One." Now we pay at usurious rates.

Even though we valiantly fight it, in our heart of hearts, we face the absolute certainty that we do not belong where we have landed. We know that we cannot repair the damage. Our health suffers. We gain or lose weight. We drink too much. We develop coping mechanisms to get through holidays and anniversaries. The family pressures to keep us together are enormous. We know that at some point we must divide the friends and family. We know that they will take sides in this division of financial and human assets. There are painful choices to be made about the custody of the pets, to say nothing about the kids.

We are relieved when our spouse is out of town or comes home late. We carve out islands of solitude, if only for a few minutes or hours. We develop a new circle of friends with whom we talk of little else but our distressed relationship. These friends are usually in a similar quandary. We have frequent conversations with them about every nuance of our situations. Our discussions are littered with heaping platitudes of bullshit: "Kids are resilient, they'll get over it," "Leopards don't change their spots," "She doesn't have my libido," "The kids will learn to be flexible having two homes."

We wake up to realize that we traded the prince or princess for a day mirage of marital Neverland for a reality that resembles Guantanamo Bay.[55] We are shackled and facing a legal fight of trench warfare proportions. The future is anything but assured and known. Our troubled relationship is our first thought upon waking. It is our last thought before we sleep. We are never at peace. We walk on eggshells not to offend our spouses. We do not want to make things worse, even temporarily. Paralyzed and rooted to the spot, we may not even know where to start if we could. In this disoriented wilderness, our compass looses its true north. The line to our primary anchor and safety in this chaotic world is cut. Everything we have built in our married life is torn asunder and called into question. We are starting to drift out to sea as if caught up in a rip tide.

Giving up brings public and private ridicule, an acknowledgement to everyone around us that we failed. We are aware that the people we publicly call our friends, will privately snicker behind our backs if we divorce. We fear their rejection; even if in our hearts we do not care what they think. We must keep up appearances and protect the myth of our perky Gap store family image. We fear the rejection of our church group, golf club or reading circle. The lie we have been living, be that of Rolex or Timex status, will be publically shattered. We are keen to avoid the inquisition of others into our human frailty. It's an interrogation that usually ends with others asking, "What was his problem? She seemed so nice." "Was he cheating?" "Was he abusive?" "Men are dogs, was he like all the rest?" or other such questions of "hanging judge" tonality.

Quietly beneath these reasons though, one factor predominates to make us stay when we know it is time to leave. Deepest down, we are afraid of the unknown. We fear being alone. Especially on weekends, we go out of our way to be invited somewhere, anywhere, with anyone, to do anything, just not to be by ourselves and have to face the fact that we have no other options. Our self-image and confidence are in the toilet. We ask ourselves tortuous questions: "How will I find someone?" "Will I grow old alone?" "How will I support myself?" "Am I still attractive?" "Will anyone want me? I am too tall (short, flat, wide)." The list of unspoken anxieties is endless. Alternatively, we may be in a complete state of denial. We ask ourselves how an untrained monkey could not see that we are completely right and our spouse is completely wrong, so strong is our ego and pride.

All of this disruption leads us to make hasty decisions. We often find a new ship on which to jump to before we abandon our sinking marital vessel. We figure out who is available for any kind of relationship.

Before we leave, we develop backup plans for future dates. We size up opportunities to meet people, even if tangentially to gain friends with benefits. We concoct inventive scenarios to make this manifest, a la the male colleague who needs to urgently discuss office business at 4:30 p.m. with a female colleague (whose husband just happens to be out of town) suggesting that the meeting be held over a drink or some other plot line. This ploy is patently transparent, but, assuming that the drink occurs, the man will know, based on the conversation and woman's body language, if she is of the "married all the time" or "married some of the time" variety. If all goes well, the little black book gets an addition or an affair begins to hasten the marriage's final act.

If we do leave, what do we most often do with our newfound freedom? We head to the bar. We get online. We get back on the horse. We do not take the time needed to gain our mental and emotional fitness. We often default to blame without sorting out what went wrong and needs to change in a future relationship. Unfortunately, we often end up right where we started; often tearfully dry heaving on our knees.

Should you stay or should you go? If you have to ask the question, you already have a serious problem, a problem counseling is unlikely to solve. Counseling, unless it has its underpinning in unconditional love and obedience to the relationship, is highly likely to fail. Even if we learn in counseling to communicate more effectively, the counseling model is partly flawed. It assumes, to one extent or another, that resolution and change are possible, that the two people want to work at improving their relationship. A couple can counsel until hell freezes over, but if one party does not want to be there, the counseling dance can go on long after the music has stopped. Negotiations go well when two parties want resolution. Problems are solved quickly with unconditional commitment. In troubled marriages, one party is often stalling, waiting for the other to throw in the towel in order to save face.

The vast majority of couples communicate well. They communicated well when they first met. They communicated well when they first got into bed. They communicated well when they decided to get married. They communicated well when they chose to have children. The problem is not the quality of their communication, quite the opposite. The problem is that each person understands every subtle nuance of the other's communication perfectly. They simply do not like what they hear and see. They do not want what is on offer from their partner. They do not want to go where the other wants to or has taken them. They revolt in a myriad of ways, with

111

conflict being only one. They believe that following the path they are on will perpetuate the bloody mess in which they now find themselves.

We cannot compromise what we truly are; we cannot negotiate what we need out of life. We cannot change what makes each of us unique. We cannot alter our life's course to do something other than our divinely inspired purpose. If we thought we bought a Ferrari when we married and instead we ended up with a Ford, no matter how much we like Fords, we will be unhappy. Thinking he or she was "this" but finding they are "that" is predictive of divorce. No counseling in the world will close the gap between the cruise we believe we signed up for and the one we are on.

People in marital conflict spend immense amounts of energy and time trying to change the other person. Try as we may, this will never, ever, work. If someone wanted to behave a certain way, they already would. In essence, our spouse would make the adjustments needed as soon as they became aware of the problem. They would not let the situation ramp up into open warfare threatening the relationship. If one person is willing to let a behavior continue while it causes pain to their spouse, the marriage is on very shaky ground. A better approach is to assure oneself before marriage, to the greatest extent possible, that the other person is on the same bus in life that we are, a bus that rides down a street of shared values and goals. If the other person is truly on the same bus, progress can be made; connection will deepen. If not, we are engaged in futility, no matter how hard we try.

At this very moment we may not be sure what marital road or bus is ours. If we are unsure of our path in life, how much time have we spent working to find it? How much quiet time have we devoted to this quest? What is more important to your long-term happiness at this moment than for you to discover where you truly belong and with whom? Are you part of a family? Do you want to be? Knowing what we want out of life and with whom we wish to share our lives is something on which we should dwell at length. We can learn much from the lives, loves, losses and blessings of others we respect. Ask them how they figured it out.

This work and reflection is something we schedule, a search to which we purposefully give our top priority over all which is optional. One does not have to travel to a distant shore to see the sunset to embark on this journey of purpose. This quest is something for which we silence our rational voices and journal on paper without limits. We write and pray until the answer appears. Writing is powerful; it commits us to action and looks back at us from the page as to its veracity.

If, after this reflection, we are not unconditionally committed to our spouse and the direction we must go with them to stay together or they are not unconditionally committed to us, this is a strong sign that we should not share the same bed and house. Love others enough to watch them leave, wish them peace and pray for their happiness. "Let go and let God." (Psalms 46:10) Moreover, if after such work you are still not sure, do nothing. Wait until the answer is unequivocal in your head, heart and the pit of your gut.

Should we stay together for the kids? No. They are the innocent pawns in a cold war of domestic attrition. Is it not better that they see, after no stone is left unturned for resolution, at least one happy, functional and healing parent rather than two dysfunctional ones? How strong of a parent can you be in the presence of an addicted and conflicted partner? While immensely challenging in the framework of a divorce, the solution is to be the best single or post-divorce parent you can be at every level in your situation. I know from firsthand experience that it can work out. I have two wonderful daughters. While nothing is perfect, collectively we did the best we could with what we had and came out the other side with love. Alana and Bianca are the fine young women that I hoped to give over to the world when they went away to college. It can work out for you too.

Chapter 6

And Finally

"Sometimes it was worth all the disadvantages of marriage just to have that: one friend in an indifferent world." (Fred R. Shapiro 407)

From the book *Fear of Flying* by Erica Jong (1942 – present) (Eleanor Mills 128)

In high school and throughout college, I wanted to be a dentist for the money. I perceived the lifestyle as glamorous as do most people outside the profession. Coming from a lower middle class family, I wanted to change my circumstance and be "free." When I was a boy I would see airplanes and wish I were in them, going anywhere. "Freedom" to me meant to travel when and where I wanted. I had an insatiable drive to get into dental school. A funny thing happened when I graduated and got out into practice as a general dentist. I hated it. I had 10 thumbs. As a result, to this day, I have immense respect for general dentists; they wear many hats: clinician, business owner, staff manager and psychologist, to name a few. Being a general dentist is a very difficult job. It only takes one orgasmic chicken in the chair to ruin the day. There are a modest number of pats on the back in this line of work. Few people come in and say how delighted they are to be there. These challenges can make old doctors out of young ones well before their time.

I was very lucky to find endodontics. The specialty fit me like a glove. I was a natural. Endodontics is artistic, scientific, helps people immediately and yet, there is finality to both its completion and clinical outcome. Over the long term, the treatment succeeds or fails; there is little middle ground. All of the above notwithstanding, I entered the specialty at a time in the early 1990's when there was massive demand for endodontists and profitability was at an all time high. Having benefited from this abundance, it was to provide me with many challenges that would later cause me to change my thinking, values and behavior.

The materialism pervasively sold to us in popular culture puzzles me. While it is seductive, it never leads to happiness. Over time, our material wealth comes to own us, not the other way around. Through worry and stress, our possessions weave a web that entangles us. The more we have, the more secure the knots. We must constantly protect what we have so as to not allow it to be taken away. An existence predicated on the financial bottom line begets a never-ending craving for more and simultaneous dissatisfaction with perceived unmet needs. Such an appetite holds no hope of satiation. Despite this, we ferociously chase more. We trade up to bigger houses, faster cars and more glamorous spouses.

When are we content? When is enough simply enough? When do we quit upsizing? When do we accept our everyday existence contains what we need to be happy? When do we give thanks to God for what we have and be pleased rather than focusing on what we believe we lack? When do we stop comparing ourselves to some rock star, actor, athlete, friend, family member or other reality that is not ours? More importantly, why do we long to be something we are not?

I have never heard a rehabilitated celebrity express remorse or responsibility for the death and destruction it took to put drugs on their table. The rural poor in Mexico and many South American countries pay in blood for our obsession with sex, drugs and rock-n-roll. Those affected in the war torn inner cities of America are not so keen either on the cost paid to fuel the rocket ride of these stars and starlets. It is ironic that we idolize such behaviors and do so with such a blind eye to the true human cost.

There is persuasive evidence that collectively we value wealth, power and instant gratification over much else in this life. As one symptom of this among many, how many marriages are tossed aside at the seven-to ten-year mark to trade in the house and spouse for a new and sexier model, a model that most often possesses a more complex set of problems? What of those people who do not fit on one side or another of the white picket fence in the Ken and Barbie American dream of personal or martial acquisition? What of the people who have been cast off, the ones who were never the prom queen or a quarterback of the football team, the rejects of a never-ending pursuit for more of everything?

I am rich because I have peace in my home with my wife and good relationships with my daughters and my wife's children; there is nothing more valuable on this earth to me. I have faith. While money is important, my happiness is determined neither by the size of my bank account nor by whether I am on magazine covers. God is for me and wants me to succeed in all things. The Bible tells me, "Though an army should encamp against me, my heart shall not fear. Though war should rise against me, even then I will be confident." (Psalm 27.3) How much more assurance do I need to know that I can prevail over my circumstance? We can all prevail and be happy if only we choose it. Happiness is a byproduct of being content with what we have and working doggedly to fix the things that need changing. At the end of the day, that is all that can be done at any given moment. In essence, we should do our best each day and sleep in peace with that affirmation.

We cannot measure our success and happiness in a freeze frame, but rather as a continuum. Our bank balance does not measure our success or our self worth. Some wealthy people are both miserable and miserly. Some with a lot fewer dollars have much bigger smiles than their wealthy counterparts. I know which of these two I would rather be. The more money I have had in life, the more exponentially complex my life became. My favorite memories and what I hold dear in my heart as the best moments of my life have all been free. In addition to the day I married Laura, one such moment was tent camping with Alana and Bianca at Smith Rock in Central Oregon teaching them to play cards by lantern light. The moment was simple, inexpensive, unplanned and perfect. I can still see their smiling faces and hear their laughter. What more do I need?

How much gold would replace Laura? What would soothe the sting of her loss? Despite my tepid rate of success, why would I put her and our nightly cribbage games at risk? What earthly pleasure or sum of money would compensate for the peace we have in our home? How we got there is another essay and perhaps something co-written, but at its essence, there is a complete submission to each other and a set of values that, at their heart, are Christian. There is no Rich first. There is no Laura first. There is no "me first." There is only "we" and "we first." This marital formula could not be simpler. All our cards are up on the table, all the time. We do not step around elephants in our living room. If something is working, we give thanks and celebrate. If something needs work, we solve it. We do not walk around with rocks in our shoes. For us, marriage, like love, is a verb. This is something we work and play at, every single day. Laura knows that I will never stomp out of the house, that I will never threaten to leave. I know the same of her. She knows that she can rely on me to work with her to sort the problem, right there, right then, no matter how painful, no matter what. We stay there until it's finished.

We abide by the Italian concept of divorce as described to me by my mother, a "gun on the mantle" variety where the only separation possible is a feet first retreat. I greatly prefer this to the "as long as we both shall choose" variety, a rendition that stresses convenience over commitment and sexual inflammation over a deeper love. This former style of marriage is usually sworn to in a three-to eight-minute ceremony in Vegas or perhaps in an up and coming trendy bar. In English football terms, Laura and I are both "stuck in." Translated, we are committed.

Finally, I love my wife for many reasons, most of which will remain private, but on this point, I will brag on her. Laura is the personification of authentic; there are no bells and whistles. Sure, she could wear them. She could wrap her persona in them. She knows though that the bling and material trappings of happiness sold to us in our culture are unnecessary. Part of what I noticed when I first saw her was her radiant gray hair. She is beautiful and desirable to me as she is. That she did not color her hair told me from the get-go that she is comfortable in her own skin. This unmistakable sign spoke volumes about her character. She had made a conscious choice to just be who she is without the props. While she certainly can dress up or down, she, not the stuff, is what I love.

Inside a calm demeanor, ours is a relationship of fire, one that would not appear to the outside world. If nothing else, our marriage is real and does not require the trappings of glitter, glamour, fame, money, power or rock stardom. We are only a man and a woman doing their best to love one another. I cannot ask for more than that. It is with her that I cast my lot and commit my future. It is with her that I "Come to Heal."

Epilogue

In September of 2009, just before this book went to print, I made another trip to cave dive in the Bahamas. The e-mail below was sent to Laura after the third of four dive days. A previous dive to this blue hole (Nancy's, which is within a mile of both Dan's and Ralph's cave systems referenced elsewhere in Dead Stuck) had to be aborted because of a poorly fitting dry suit. Nancy's blue hole contains the skeleton bones of Lucayan Indians and one "grinder restriction" of the type in which I had gotten myself dead stuck. The e-mail appears here exactly as it was written.

"Today was special... Wow, I won't forget today for a long time... I could write a book about it...

The first dive was the blue hole where the lucayan skeleton leg bones were from the last trip that I had to abort because the dry suit didn't fit... the carry to the blue hole from the road is probably 175 yards through the brush... the cover to the blue hole is about half the size of our kitchen, if that... and its overgrown with vegetation... Brian had to machete a fair bit of the vegetation out of the hole to get us room to get in... The hydrogen sulfide layer at the top, aside from smelling nasty, was pretty thick and as black as oil. The talis (debris mound at the entrance) was immense for such a small hole... anyway, this cave had it all... We descended into total darkness even with the lights due to the sulfide layer...it really was like going through oil... only the line showed me the way down initially. On the dive we got to go through some massive speliothems...very impressive crystal formations, one looked like a steam ship that was twice the height of the Range Rover and just as long and wide... anyway, we came upon a grinder restriction at which I had the option of calling the dive (i.e. turning around) or going through... it was small. I didn't have to take a tank off but it was the smallest thing I've been through since getting dead stuck. As I approached, I kept telling myself I could stop at any time and when I was at the point of no return I just put my head down and pulled myself through over the length (feeling the cave on all sides of me) of it which was at least 20 feet... coming out it was close to zero visibility because of the muck we stirred up going in... I just closed my eyes and thought positive thoughts until I was through... I literally cried from joy under my mask when I was free of it. My dead stuck demons had left me... I felt blessed to be there and grateful to God for giving me the courage and strength not to turn back and quit... I've been queasy about restrictions since *Dead Stuck* occurred and this was a great first step in getting over it. The rest of the dive was marked with minor problems with my BC trapping air and not letting me float with the right trim... this is a new problem... we'll get it sorted... Saw the Lucayan skeleton leg bones... big dude... he doesn't need them now. Brian also found some additional tortoise vertebrae down there... another extinguished species.

Second dive was in Ralphs in the pretty section that will be in the Nat geo special. The esthetics of this dive defy superlatives and description. If you only did one cave dive in your life this would be it. Interestingly, before the dive there was a torrential rain and lightning and thunderstorm... impressive. Ironic to be in a wet suit waiting in a downpour in the middle of the forest waiting for it to clear so Brian could walk his tanks to the hole... The variety and sheer volume of amazing crystal in Ralphs cannot be overstated. When I said this was Gods most beautiful creation (besides you), I meant it.

One thing I saw today, that I had never seen before were a series of crystals that resembled little plants. They had clear crystal bottoms about 2 inches wide in circumference at their base. Emerging out of the crystal bases were numerous red spikes sticking out about another inch... they were like the leaves that emerge from a pineapple, just as numerous but much thinner. If I had not seen them underwater, I would swear that these were small flowers or plants blown in the finest glass shop in the world... and priceless ones at that...the dive went well.

Tomorrow is a double stage dive to the far end of Wrigley Field beyond Fangorn forest... I/we will be careful. I love you. Will call later after dinner... kisses... Rich"

Appendix A:

Q&A: "The Overhead Environment"

When people ask me what I do for a living and I reply "root canals" their first words are usually, "Oh Ouch!" This tends to be a short conversation. By contrast, when they ask me about my hobbies, I say "scuba diving in caves" which draws puzzled looks and probing questions. Some of these are answered below. This provides additional context to the story "Dead Stuck at 123 Feet Underwater."

Q: *"What makes cave diving different from open water scuba?"*

A: Scuba diving in caves, at the highest level of technical difficulty, is as far removed from open water recreational diving as Formula 1 is from Go Karts. They are both motorized vehicles, but that is where the similarity ends. Cave diving is scuba, but it is a sport played at a completely different level than open water recreational diving.

Divers in open water can ascend directly as needed in an emergency. Cave diving is gravely dangerous relative to recreational scuba because the diver cannot ascend directly to the surface at will. The cave ceiling prevents direct ascent. Without direct access to the surface, for navigational purposes, the diver must lay or have a continuous guideline (defined below) from the cave entrance to the planned point of exit. In open water, out is up. In a cave, out can be thousands of linear feet through divergent topography. This distinction is a matter of life and death seriousness should a cave dive need to be aborted in an emergency.

Cave divers generally enter and exit the water at the same location. If, for example, divers travel 1,500 feet into a cave system, to exit, unless planned otherwise, they must retrace the same route to where they entered. Exiting the cave safely requires expert buoyancy, flawless navigational skills, attention to cave topography and careful management of gas supplies. Exiting also entails uneventfully squeezing back out through any small passages (restrictions) that were traversed on the entry.

Q: *"Do people cave dive alone?"*

A: Yes. Many cave divers prefer to dive alone. If I lived near caves, I would solo cave dive at every opportunity. One rationale for solo cave diving is that the only thing worse than one fatality is two. The thread of thinking among elite cave divers is that if a diver is foolish or unlucky enough to get into trouble, why should the life of a second person also be risked trying to save them? Solo diving is the epitome of self-reliance. Alone, in a cave underwater, irrespective of the depth, there is no way to request help. Unless gas cylinders were cached previously and within reach, whatever you went in with is what you have to get yourself out.

A team of divers moving through a cave is not unlike a slithering snake. The dive team is reliant on its first diver to not silt out the cave with poor buoyancy technique as well as to identify the correct route both inbound and outbound. Turning a team of divers around if the lead diver makes a wrong turn or because the dive must be aborted does not happen on a dime. Among other considerations, its efficiency depends on the number of team members, emergency at hand and cave topography. On a group cave dive, since the team members cannot speak underwater, communication takes place through a series of hand and light signals, touch contact between divers and possibly written notes. As a result, it may not be immediately obvious to team members what problem someone may be having.

While there are benefits in numbers, solo diving greatly simplifies the activity. It eliminates variables, accidents and potential errors. For example, what if a team member ignores directional markers or turns the wrong way? What if you are diving with a buddy and he or she has a heart attack, catastrophic gear failure, gets lost and cannot be found or must be left for other reasons such as getting dead stuck? When viewed in this light, solo cave diving is much more rational than it would otherwise first appear.

Q: *"How do you know where you are at any given time?"*

A: Previously explored caves have guidelines. These lines are the "highway" into and out of the cave. Each major passage has it own guideline. Guidelines have markers, known as line arrows that tell the diver the direction and distance of the nearest exit. Off of the main guidelines there are secondary guidelines, close to but not connected with the main guideline. These lines take the diver into branches off the main cave passage. To move from the main line to the secondary line, the diver carries reels of additional line and makes a "jump" from the main line to the secondary line.

As mentioned, it is of vital importance for the diver to maintain a continuous guideline from the entrance of the cave. Cave systems have an astonishing diversity of tunnels, branches and geologic features. The guideline and directional markers are an essential navigational aid, especially if the diver becomes disoriented or visibility is lost. The diver should be within arm's reach of the guideline at all times, an ideal that is neither practical nor possible in all cave topography. Guidelines can be read manually if necessary, almost like reading Braille should visibility drop to zero. If interpreted correctly, the directional line markers can guide the diver to their exit.

Such poor or zero visibility can result from poor finning technique, especially in smaller cave passages where it is possible to kick up silt (mud, sand, clay) from the cave floor with just a few misplaced fin kicks. Even with dive torches equivalent to a BMW headlight, if there is no appreciable current in the passage, stirred up silt from the cave floor can eliminate visibility for hours. Some cave passages are so silty and restricted that is it impossible to move within them without a total and rapid loss of visibility.

In an emergency compounded by zero visibility, one's life literally depends on maintaining contact with the line and "reading" its directional markers accurately. If a diver loses contact with the line in zero visibility, their life is truly at risk. Imagine the horror of being sightless and hitting the cave wall without any idea of the way forward. Amazingly, explorers routinely work in zero visibility when moving through small virgin spaces trying to connect one cave system with another or to determine the length of a cave that has not yet been fully explored.

A story related to me by an experienced cave diver is instructive. One diver cut a guideline to free himself from a line entanglement after silting out a passage and by doing so left his buddy, who was further distant in the cave (away from the entrance) with no way to determine which way was up, down or out in zero visibility. Making matters worse, the second diver had to move through a restriction to attempt to find the cut guideline in the mud. This scenario is much worse than a blizzard. At least in a whiteout, it is clear which way is up. Not so in zero visibility in a cave. Fortunately, the endangered diver was able to find the cut end of the line in the mud and exit the cave alive. A less than cordial reunion occurred above water between the divers when the second surfaced to find the first having lunch with no intention of offering an apology. Had the second diver panicked, this scenario could have easily led to his death.

Q: *"Is it dark down there?"*

A: Yes, and how. Once past the cavern zone, inside the cave, without lights, there is total darkness. Divers start a cave dive in the cavern zone. The cavern zone is the area of the cave possessing some visible light even if it may be the faintest glow of perceptible illumination generally no more than 200 feet from the surface. Even though being close to the entrance is intuitively "safer," this is not necessarily true. Even though the diver might be very close to the surface in linear feet, it may neither be obvious nor intuitive where they might look to see the light in an unfamiliar cave, hence emphasizing the importance of a guideline to direct them.

Cave divers should carry three lights at all times, a primary light (larger and more powerful) and two backups (smaller and less powerful). It is highly improbable that all three lights will fail on the same dive. Even if all three lights became inoperable at the same time, if diving in a group, a team member would lend a light, or, if the diver were solo diving, the guideline could be followed manually to the entrance in darkness.

I once went on a cave dive and forgot to put on my diving helmet. Helmets are often worn to prevent the diver from hitting their heads on the cave's rock ceiling. My two backup lights are attached to my helmet. On a different dive, I once failed to fully seal the battery canister on my primary dive light. The primary light failed after flooding several minutes into the dive. Had I made both mistakes on the same dive and been alone, I could have easily ended up in total darkness and been required to use the guideline to exit.

Q: *"What do you see down there?"*

A: The most beautiful landscapes I have witnessed on earth are in the caves I have had the privilege to dive. Words alone cannot describe the beauty of these hallowed sanctuaries. This is God's handiwork at its best. There is a room inside Dan's Cave (Abacos, Bahamas) literally the width of Wrigley Field in Chicago. Aptly named Wrigley Field, it is next to a colossal room known as Fangorn Forest. The floor of Wrigley Field resembles the moon's surface. Close to the entrance to Wrigley Field in Fangorn Forest, there are three mammoth crystal towers made of calcite over 30 feet high, 20 feet or more in width and 15 to 20 feet in depth horizontally. These formations undulate vertically like the robe of a priest to a depth in which I can insert my hand up to my elbow. Light projects fully through the undulating translucent white crystal sections of the robe. I call these three towers the "Three Apostles." Formally, they are known as the "Three Ents" from *The Lord of the Rings*. These crystalline formations were created in the Pleistocene epoch[56] during glacial periods from water that seeped through the ground strata to evaporate in what was then dry cave. (Fairchild) The walls of Fangorn Forest have crystal formations that ripple like frozen waterfalls, hugely oversized wedding cakes and church organs.

Fangorn Forest itself is literally a forest of individual stalactites and stalagmites very much like the Saguaro National Forest near Tucson, Arizona. Like a true forest, these crystal formations are often so thick that they cannot be seen through. Rising from the cave floor or descending from the ceiling, these crystals are anywhere from the size of a soda straw to the giants mentioned above. Some formations, like the Three Apostles, literally extend the entire vertical height of the room. The room's ceiling is covered with an infinite number of vertical crystals of varying lengths that have taken the shape of delicate flowers, angel wings, fishhooks and letters. Many of these terminate in multi surface smooth and symmetrical shapes ranging from the size of a pea to an oversized softball.

Throughout Dan's Cave, it is possible to glide over bathtub size pools that contain countless geometric (often hexagonal) crystals of varying heights. Some pools also contain crystals that resemble symmetrical twelve sided flower buds that are as much as seven inches at their widest dimension. One formation is especially intriguing, a hollow yet perfectly symmetrical amber donut resembling a tire, approximately two feet in diameter, which lies flat on the cave floor and yet is completely covered (inside and out) with geometric crystal shapes.

Ralph's Cave, the adjoining cave system next to Dan's, has rooms of such crystal decoration that divers must literally pull themselves by their fingertips in order to glide within an inch or two over the floor. With formations above and to each side of the diver, the smallest loss of buoyancy control will easily cause the diver in an instant to break crystals that took eons to form. Shining one's dive light into the innumerable soda straw projections creates a menagerie of reflecting light evocative of hundreds of continuously shooting stars.

Some cave floors within Dan's resemble a flood plain during drought. Clay and mud on the cave floor remain from when the cave was dry during the glacial periods of the Pleistocene epoch and retain a bronze color, a remnant of dust that was blown at that time across the globe from the Sahara Desert. When the cave filled with water after the end of the last ice age approximately 10,000 to 11,000 years ago, the cracking mud retained its sharp lines of demarcation as if the separation and drying occurred yesterday. Both these cracks and crystals will remain as they are until the next climatic shift, at which time the floor will dry out again and new crystals will be created through the same evaporation.

This passage, written by Agnes Milowka and taken from *Underwater Speleology*, the Journal of the National Speleological Society Cave Diving Section, speaks to the beauty of these two cave systems (Dan's and Ralphs, Abaco's, Bahamas): "Yet, at the end of the day I am a cave diver and, as far as I'm concerned the pursuit of extraordinary beauty is a perfectly legitimate quest. The team, spearheaded by Brian Kakuk,[57] headed to a couple of beautiful caves called Dan's and Ralph's to photograph and film them. Dan's was my first opportunity to see speleothems underwater, and oh boy, did I get spoiled.

I was blown away to put it mildly. The sheer amount of decoration was incredible; there was room after room of decorations. Yet each room was very different and had a wildly distinct feel. My favourite was called the Alleyway, where I got to swim through a passageway with tall stalactites and stalagmites on either side of me, it felt like I was swimming through a giant crystal forest. The whole scene was illuminated from all sides by the ever-powerful Dive Rite 50W lights, meaning I could see everything - amazing!

I thought Dan's was the best cave in the world until I dove Ralph's. This cave defies description; it is probably the prettiest and most special cave on the planet. I could happily dive this cave every day for the rest of my life and not get bored with it. After you dive it, you seriously consider never setting foot inside a cave again, or perhaps simply lying down to die because nothing will ever beat this experience. Every type of crystal decoration imaginable is present in this cave; intricate rose-like formations, exquisite crystals, stalactites piled on so thick not even a flathead could swim through them without making contact. Then there were the soda straws with little diamond-shaped crystals at the tips. They say diamonds are forever, well, this cave has captured my heart big time. I felt as fuzzy as the halocline that surrounded us as we explored and photographed the caves." (Milowka)

Q: *"How deep is it?"*

A: All things being equal, depth is not the primary danger in cave diving. Rather, it is one of a host of technical considerations that is taken into account in dive planning. Caves vary greatly in depth from a minimal 20 to 30 feet to hundreds of feet (300 or more). With many exceptions, most cave divers are diving in the range of 30-150 feet. 10 feet deep is very shallow in scuba diving terms. However, 10 feet deep is extreme if the diver cannot ascend freely, has lost visibility, is disorientated or is running out of air.

Q: *"What makes cave diving so dangerous?"*

A: Drowned cave divers have been found with their fingers abraded off to their knuckles from trying to dig their way through the cave ceiling. Drowning in a cave is a horrific way to die. The diver knows exactly what is happening, literally to their last breath, mutilated fingers or not.

My first cave diving instructor told me in strong a New York accent, the overhead environment can "keel (kill) you" as he recounted how some of his friends had been killed and injured. I believe him. His mantra is now mine. Interestingly, there are older technical divers who have stopped entirely because many of their peers have either died or had severe decompression sickness, often more than once. Other cave diving veterans stopped diving because everyone they trusted to go diving with had died while diving. Billie Deans, a famous diver, had to leave one of his best friends who had become severely entangled in the SS *Andrea Doria*.[58] He no longer dives. (McMurray 273) Imagine having to swim away from your best friend knowing you, being their only hope, must depart to save yourself. The hazards of technical wreck diving are every bit as real as those in a cave.

According a cave dive the seriousness and preparation it deserves mitigates, to some degree, the dangers related here. The primary dangers of cave diving are related to losing ones orientation in the cave, neither planning nor managing gas consumption appropriately[59] and not maintaining a continuous guideline to the surface from the entrance point. All of these primary dangers, among a host of other potential secondary challenges, are diver dependent and unrelated to bad luck.

Dive planning is critical. Among many considerations, before any cave dive (recreational up to exploration level) the diver should determine the amount and optimal gas to breathe (assuming the diver is not using a rebreather[60]), the risk of narcosis (detailed below), decompression obligations[61] and oxygen toxicity.[62]

Nitrogen narcosis is the cheapest, fastest and most potentially lethal (and legal) way to get high available today. The risk of narcosis occurs with increasing time and depth depending on the chosen gas mixture. Assuming that the diver is breathing ambient air (79 percent nitrogen and 21 percent oxygen) for example, as the diver descends and absorbs more nitrogen into their bloodstream, due to the increased pressure, at some threshold, the increased dissolved nitrogen results in narcosis. Narcosis can be lethal because such mental impairment is the last thing a diver wants, especially in a cave when they most need their mental acuity. Different divers have different susceptibilities to narcosis based on a wide variety of factors.

Many divers learn to deal with narcosis through experience and mental disciple. Narcosis runs the gamut from a feeling of general well being, not unlike having a cocktail, to being absolutely stoned and seeing God while hearing what deep air diving aficionados call the "Wah Wahs." I had one such spiritual experience at 218 feet while diving on air. Narcosis on a night dive ramps up the voltage to this foreshadowing of Jesus' omnipresent love. If I said I had seen Elvis and Jimi, it would not be far from the truth. This said, I am a rank amateur, I know divers who have gone much deeper on air (well over 350 feet) and lived to tell the tale.

Cave diving tasks, hazards and variables populate a very long list. Divers can easily become "task loaded." During a dive, there are many jobs that do or could need attention. Among many, these include: laying lines (using reels), referencing the cave mentally throughout the execution of the dive plan, monitoring one's dive computer for decompression obligations and oxygen saturation-PO_2, buoyancy control, the location and status of other dive team members, rate of gas consumption and recognizing equipment malfunctions when they occur (blown "O" rings and gear trauma). Additional realistic challenges include getting tangled in the guideline, a fin falling off or having a rock projection catch a dangling piece of gear in a tightly confined space.

The cave itself ultimately determines dive planning. Dive planning takes into consideration the type of cave system (spring, siphon, ocean-tidal, fresh water, mixed ocean and fresh), composition of the cave wall and its fragility, halocline (a mixture of fresh and salt water that reduces visibility), thermocline (a mixture of warm and cold water that reduces visibility) and the risk of silt out. Moving through a halocline, for example, the dive team will swim more slowly and be staggered across the cave (as opposed to following one another in a line) to optimize visibility for divers further back from the team leader.

Navigational challenges occur. Directional markers on the guidelines may be moved, either accidently or by malice. The permutations of possible navigational mistakes is staggering in the overhead environment. What if a diver places a directional marker in the wrong place and is unfamiliar with the cave? What if the diver places the right directional marker in the right place on the entry, but on the exit the same diver interprets this marker incorrectly? In either event, disorientation, even for a moment, requires a cool head to either retrace needed steps or to read existing guideline markers and make proper directional adjustments.

One of my dive gurus told me that people lose IQ points underwater. This is true. Mistakes equivalent to locking one's keys in their car can be fatal in a cave. There are an infinite number of ways that a cave dive can go wrong. One poor decision in this unique and harsh environment can be deadly. As one example among many real fatality scenarios, I am aware of an instance where four divers ignored or missed a directional marker pointing them to their exit and instead they moved farther into the cave. Of the four divers, two perished as a result of this navigational mistake. Despite the initial error, the four divers at one point were very close to a second exit point that they knew was present but were unable to find. Retracing their path, two divers ran out of air, the two survivors literally came back on fumes.

Q: *"Aren't there guides that can keep you safe?"*

A: Yes, and no. There are many excellent guides around the world; I've been blessed to dive with several of the very best. This said, a cave diver should never rely on someone else to get him or her out of a cave. There are no "trust me" dives. "Trust me" equals "get dead." Over the long term, your number is coming up with such a mentality.

As mentioned in the story text, scuba divers do not start out cave diving. Cave diving is a sport that is slowly worked up to, ideally after hundreds of open water dives. It is unrealistic to expect that an open water diver would be ready for cave certification training unless they were expert in open water. Cave diving certification is mentally and physically challenging, much more so than open water certification. The further that the diver goes beyond the basic level of cave training with increasing numbers of dives, the more reflexive the responses to challenges that may arise during a dive.

On a final cautionary note, with lethal consequences some guides have developed poorly conceived dive plans that have left clients alone in unfamiliar caves and cavern zones with the expectation that they will be able to exit the cave unassisted. This is a recipe for disaster.

Ultimately, a guide is just that, a guide, not a service provider who is expected to eliminate all risk from the dive or carry their clients out of the cave in an emergency. In cave and technical dive training, there is a maxim, "Only I can think for me. Only I can breathe for me. Only I can swim for me." (Kevin Gurr) It is true.

Appendix B: References

1985: Uefa bans English clubs from Europe. 11 June 2009 <http://news.bbc.co.uk/onthisday/hi/dates/stories/june/2/newsid_2494000/2494963.stm>.

1989: Football fans crushed at Hillsborough. 5 June 2009 <http://news.bbc.co.uk/onthisday/hi/dates/stories/april/15/newsid_2491000/2491195.stm>.

1995: Cantona banned over attack on fan. 9 June 2009 <http://news.bbc.co.uk/onthisday/hi/dates/stories/january/27/newsid_2506000/2506237.stm>.

A History of The Premier League. 12 June 2009. <http://www.premierleague.com/page/History/0,,12306,00.html>.

A potted history of QPR 1882-2009. 3 June 2009. 6 June 2009 <http://www.qpr.co.uk/page/History/0,,10373,00.html>.

About EV-K2-CNR. 9 June 2009 <http://www.evk2cnr.org/cms/en/evk2cnr_committee/presentation/>.

Alexander Solzhenitsyn dies at 89. 4 August 2008. 16 June 2009 <http://news.bbc.co.uk/2/hi/europe/7540038.stm>.

Bad Company, Straight Shooter, 1975, "Shooting Star". 1 June 2009 <http://www.google.com/musicl?lid=XxL8fEMLVLG&aid=AfsmbKT82eL>.

Bandits 2001. 3 June 2009 <http://www.imdb.com/title/tt0219965/quotes>.

Beckham forgives Ferguson. 2003 February 19. 5 June 2009 <http://news.bbc.co.uk/sport2/hi/football/teams/m/man_utd/2778353.stm>.

Bhikkhu, Thanissaro. Samsara. 2002. 8 June 2009 <http://www.esolibris.com/articles/buddhism/samsara.php>.

Black, G.V. "Limitations of Dental Education." Dental Digest XIII (1907): 862 - 876.

Boom Boom by Pat Travers. 8 June 2009 <http://www.pattravers.com/pt/discog/2000boomboom.htm>.

Butler-Bowdon, Tom. 50 Success Classics: Winning Wisdom for Life and Work from 50 Landmark Books. London: Nicholas Brealey Publishing, 2004.

Captain William Bligh. 8 June 2009 <http://www.plantexplorers.com/explorers/biographies/captain/captain-william-bligh.htm>.

Chesterton, G.K. "The Complete "Father Brown" - The Innocence of Father Brown: The Blue Cross." University of Adelaide E-Books. 4 June 2009 <http://ebooks.adelaide.edu.au/c/chesterton/gk/c52fb/>.

Corliss, Richard. Katherine Hepburn 1907 - 2003. 6 July 2003. 16 June 2009   <http://www.time.com/time/magazine/article/0,9171,463117,00.html>.

Cristina Fernández de Kirchner. 2009. 26 June 2009 <http://www.britannica.com/EBchecked/topic/1100708/Cristina-Fernandez-de-Kirchner>.

Davies, Chris. Strachan due south as Gray loses his way. 21 October 2001. 30 July 2009 <http://www.telegraph.co.uk/sport/football/leagues/leagueone/southampton/3015229/Strachan-due-south-as-Gray-loses-his-way.html>.

Deep Purple, "Machine Head", 1972. 19 July 2009. <http://www.google.com/musicl?lid=x2M3eWNgtBC&aid=f_6J-_lpxWN>.

Diego Maradona goal voted the FIFA World Cup™ Goal of the Century. 30 May 2002. 9 June 2009 <http://www.fifa.com/newscentre/news/news-id=82406.html>.

Drama Across Planet Football. 19 Febuary 2009. 12 June 2009 <http://www.fifa.com/worldfootball/clubfootball/news/newsid=1028638.html>.

Edith Wharton, 75, Is Dead in France. 13 August 1937. 16 June 2009 <http://www.nytimes.com/learning/general/onthisday/bday/0124.html>.

Eleanor Mills, Kira Cochrane. Journalistas: 100 years of the Best Writing and Reporting by Women Journalists. New York: Carroll & Graf Publishers, 2005.

Esar, Evan. 20,000 Quips and Quotes. New York: Barnes and Noble Publishing, 1995.

Fairchild, I.J., Frisia, S., Borsato, A. and Tooth, A.F. "Speleothems." Dr. David J. Nash, Sue J. McLaren (. Geochemical Sediments and Landscapes. Oxford: Blackwell Publishing, 2007. 200 - 246.

Fountain, John W. 3 Die as Scaffolding Falls From Chicago Skyscraper. 10 March 2002. 25 June 2009 <http://www.nytimes.com/2002/03/10/us/3-die-as-scaffolding-falls-from-chicago-skyscraper.html>.

Fred R. Shapiro, Joseph Epstein. The Yale book of Quotations. New Haven: Yale University Press, 2006.

Free, All Right Now, 1970. 30 July 2009 <http://www.google.com/musicl?lid=KNCPvRMLM9C&aid=mG2imnDG8zF>.

George Latimer Apperson, M. Manser. Wordsworth Dictionary of Proverbs . Ware: Wordsworth Editions, ltd. , 2003.

German fans thank team in mass celebration. 30 July 2009 <http://www.stararticle.com/article_111986_German-fans-thank-team-in-mass-celebration.html>.

Glazer wins control of Man United. 12 Mat 2005. 3 June 2009 <http://news.bbc.co.uk/2/hi/business/4540939.stm>.

Google Music: Bad Company, 10 from 6, 1985. 1 June 2009 <http://www.google.com/musicl?lid=3m0TBJ8rxaE&aid=AfsmbKT82eL>.

Greenberg, Amy S. Talk of the Past - Americans in the Tropics. October 2005. 24 June 2009 <http://www.common-place.org/vol-06/no-01/talk/>.

Haggard, H. Rider. King Solomon's Mines. New York: Barnes and Noble Classics, 2004.

Hale, Briony. Bankruptcy fears hit football. 6 May 2001. 2009 <http://news.bbc.co.uk/2/hi/business/1312650.stm>.

Hamilton, Gavin. 50 sporting things you must do before you die. Ed. Gordon Thomson. 4 April 2004. 28 July 2009 <http://observer.guardian.co.uk/osm/story/0,6903,1182710,00.html>.

Hansen, Jack Canfield and Mark Victor. The Aladdin Factor. NY: Berkley Books, 1995.

Higham, Nicholas J. MATLAB guide. Natick: The MatchWorks Inc., 2005.

Irvine, A. D. Bertrand Russell. 1 May 2003. 16 June 2009 <http://plato. stanford.edu/entries/russell/>.

Isle of Wight Festival History 1969. 9 June 2009 <http://www.isleofwight-festival.com/history/1969.aspx>.

James Dart, Paul Doyle and Jon Hill. The greatest rags-to-riches stories ever. 12 April 2006. 8 June 2009 <http://www.guardian.co.uk/football/2006/apr/12/theknowledge.sport>.

James McMurty, It Had to Happen, 1997. 30 Juky 2009 <http://www.google.com/musicl?lid=tT_hpvvWztL&aid=NFxsUpywgHF>.

James, Stuart. Manchester United alone hit loyal fans with season-ticket price increase. 23 April 2009. 5 June 2009 <http://www.guardian.co.uk/football/2009/apr/23/manchester-united-premier-league-season-tickets>.

Johnson, Samuel. Rasselas. Oxford: Oxford University Press, 1999.

—. Samuel Johnson, 1709-1784: a list of books with references to periodicals in the Brooklyn public library. New York: Brooklyn Public Library, 1909.

Karakoram Range. 2009. 7 July 2009 <http://www.britannica.com/EBchecked/topic/312055/Karakoram-Range>.

Kevin Gurr, Tom Mount. Trimix Student Workbook. Miami Shores: The International Association of Nitrox and Technical Divers/IANTD, 1998.

Keyes, Ralph. The Quote Verifier: Who Said What, Where, and When. New York: Macmillan, 2006.

Klinnsman Pays Tribute to Players. 8 July 2008. 3 June 2009 <http://news.bbc.co.uk/sport2/hi/football/world_cup_2006/teams/germany/5152718.stm>.

Krieger, Richard Alan. Civilization's Quotations: Life's Ideal. New York: Algora Publishing, 2002.

Kumar, M. Dictionary of Quotations. New Dehli: APH Publishing, n.d.

Loh, Sandra Tsing. "Let's Call the Whole Thing Off." July 2009. The Atlantic Online. 6 July 2009 <http://www.theatlantic.com/doc/200907/divorce>.

Lukacs, John. A Thread of Years. New Haven: Yale University Press, 1999.

Man Utd complete Berbatov switch. 1 September 2008. 5 June 2009 <http://news.bbc.co.uk/sport2/hi/football/eng_prem/7592272.stm>.

Man Utd thump Celtic. 23 Juky 2003. 5 June 2009 <http://news.bbc.co.uk/sport2/hi/football/3086949.stm>.

McHugh, Deborah. The Quotable Traveler. Guilford: Globe Pequot, 2001.

McMurray, Kevin F. Deep Descent: Adventure and Death Diving the Andrea Doria. New York: Touchstone, 2001.

Melville, Herman. Moby Dick. London: CRW Publishing Limited, 2004.

Milowka, Agnes. "Deep Holes: Unraveling the Mysteries of the Bahamas." Underwater Speleology July/August/September 2009: 12 - 14.

Musial, Mike Eisenbath and Stan. The Cardinals Encyclopedia. Philadelphia: Temple University Press, 1999.

Nabokov, Vladimir. Lolita. New York: Random House, 1997.

Nietzsche, Friedrich Wilhelm. Ecce Homo: How One Becomes What One Is. Trans. R. J. Hollingdale. London: Penguin Classics, 1992.

Ogden, Mark. Manchester United accept £80m bid for Cristiano Ronaldo from Real Madrid. 11 June 2009. 16 July 2009 <http://www.telegraph.co.uk/sport/football/leagues/premierleague/manutd/5503288/Manchester-United-accept-80m-bid-for-Cristiano-Ronaldo-from-Real-Madrid.html>.

Old Firm's enduring appeal. 12 February 2009. 5 June 2009 <http://www.fifa.com/classicfootball/news/newsid=1023776.html>.

Pesonen, Petri Liukkonen & Ari. Jean De LA Fontaine. 2008. 24 June 2009 <http://www.kirjasto.sci.fi/fontaine.htm>.

Pleistocene Epoch. 2009. 27 June 2009 <http://encarta.msn.com/encyclopedia_761573397/Pleistocene_Epoch.html>.

Power, Paddy. Wembley Stadium, can we fix it? Er, well, sorry, no we can't, actually . . . 25 February 2005. 2009 July 2009 <http://www.timesonline.co.uk/tol/sport/football/article734676.ece>.

"Premier League Handbook 2008/09: Rules." 2008. Premier League. 5 June 2009 <http://www.premierleague.com/staticFiles/7a/20/0,,12306~139386,00.pdf>.

Premier League History: Season 1995/96. 5 June 2009 <http://www.premierleague.com/page/1995/96Season>.

Prochnow, Herbert Victor. The New Speaker's Treasury of Wit and Wisdom. New York: Harper and Row, 1958.

Queiroz urges Ronaldo to stay put. 2008 24 June. 5 June 2009 <http://news.bbc.co.uk/sport2/hi/football/teams/m/man_utd/7463439.stm>.

Reaction to Keane's retirement. 12 June 2006. 5 June 2009 <http://news.bbc.co.uk/sport2/hi/football/5072152.stm>.

Real top Man Utd in rich league. 14 February 2008. 5 June 2009 <http://news.bbc.co.uk/2/hi/business/7242490.stm>.

Ribstein, Max. G.K. Chesterton (1874-1936): création romanesque et imagination. Ann Arbor: University of Michigan, 1981.

Richard W. Thorington, Katie Ferrell. Squirrels: The Animal Answer Guide. Baltimore: John Hopkins University Press, 2006.

Russel, Bertrand. Marriage and Morals. New York: Routledge Classic, 2009.

Scarface. 23 July 2009 <http://www.imdb.com/title/tt0086250/quotes>.

Shannon, William V. We Who Left Ireland. 1 December 1985. 30 July 2009 <http://www.nytimes.com/1985/12/01/books/we-who-left-ireland.html?sec=&spon=&pagewanted=all>.

Sherry Sontag, Christopher Drew, Annette Lawrence Drew. Blind Man's Bluff: the Untold Story of American Submarine Espionage. New York: Public Affairs, 1998.

Sir Alex Ferguson. 5 June 2009 <http://www.manutd.com/default.sps?pagegid=%7bA92398BD-4211-402B-B90A-BF0DE2924904%7d&section=playerProfile&teamid=&bioid=91976>.

Slot, Owen. The Sporting Power 100. 2009 January 24. 2009 <http://www.timesonline.co.uk/tol/sport/more_sport/article5576544.ece?token=null&offset=24&page=3>.

Smith, Rory. Manchester City's Mark Hughes insists he has full backing of club's Arab owners. 20 March 2009. 16 June 2009 <http://www.telegraph.co.uk/sport/football/leagues/premierleague/mancity/5011926/Manchester-Citys-Mark-Hughes-insists-he-has-full-backing-of-clubs-Arab-owners.html>.

Solhekol, Kaveh. Manchester United accept £80 million offer from Real Madrid for Cristiano Ronaldo. 11 June 2009. 17 June 2009 <http://www.timesonline.co.uk/tol/sport/football/premier_league/manchester_united/article6476897.ece>.

Sorensen, Soren. Northwest 1981. 22 August 2001. 3 June 2009 <http://www.phys.utk.edu/sorensen/cfr/cfr/Output/1981/CF_1981_Team_Northwestern.html>.

Spaaij, Ramn. Understanding Football Hooliganism a Comparison of Six Western European Football Clubs. Amsterdam: Amsterdam University Press, 2006.

Spanton, Tim. Film Star Cantona. 5 May 2009. 23 July 2009 <http://www.thesun.co.uk/sol/homepage/features/article2411677.ece>.

Taylor, Rt Hon Lord Justice. The Hillsborough Stadium Disaster. Parliamentary. London: Home Office, 1989.

The Clash, Combat Rock, 1982. 30 July 2009 <http://www.google.com/musicl?lid=MXdklFErKjD&aid=-ndXFXJEdsG>.

The club since 1878. 5 June 2009 <http://www.manutd.com/default.sps?pagegid={E0DB31FD-0C0E-49D7-98B7-AA7B75FF0E21}>.

The Heysel disaster. 29 May 2000. 5 June 2009 <http://news.bbc.co.uk/2/hi/uk_news/768380.stm>.

The Life and Times of Eric Cantona. 27 January 1995. 9 June 2009 <http://www.independent.co.uk/sport/the-life-and-times-of-eric-cantona-1570034.html>.

The Life of Hellen Keller. 20 November 2008. 16 June 2009 <http://www.rnib.org.uk/xpedio/groups/public/documents/publicwebsite/public_keller.hcsp>.

The Mutiny on HMS Bounty. 2002. 30 July 2009 <http://www.royalnavalmuseum.org/info_sheets_bounty.htm>.

The Presidents . 16 June 2009 <http://www.whitehouse.gov/about/presidents/harrystruman/>.

UEFA Club Football Awards. 22 August 2008. 5 June 2009 <http://www.uefa.com/competitions/supercup/finals/newsid=559183.html>.

Wallace, Sam. Football: Manchester United's academy old boys. 18 March 2008. 5 June 2009 <http://blogs.independent.co.uk/extratime/2008/03/football-manche.html>.

Walter Mitty. 8 June 2009 <http://dictionary.reference.com/browse/walter%20mitty>.

Weldon, Roger. Living the Abundant Life. Longwood: Xulon Press, 2004.

Westwood, Ben. Manchester: The Theatre of Dreams. 2004 4 September. 2009 June 2009 <http://www.telegraph.co.uk/travel/activityandadventure/724989/Manchester-The-Theatre-of-Dreams.html>.

White, Duncan. <u>Cristiano Ronaldo wins Fifa World Player of the Year</u>. 2008 12 January. 5 June 2009 <http://www.telegraph.co.uk/sport/football/cristianoronaldo/4224600/Cristiano-Ronaldo-wins-Fifa-World-Player-of-the-Year.html>.

Whiteside, Kelly. <u>German coach makes long commute</u>. 7 December 2005. 5 June 2009 <http://www.usatoday.com/sports/soccer/world/2005-12-07-klinsmann-cover_x.htm>.

Wikes, William. <u>Soccer and The Spanish Civil War</u>. 6 Feb 2008. 5 June 2009 <http://spanish-history.suite101.com/article.cfm/soccer_and_the_spanish_civil_war>.

Wolff, Cynthia Griggin. <u>A Feast of Words: The Triumph of Edith Wharton</u>. Oxford: Oxford University Press, 1977.

Wolfgang Mieder, Stewart A. Kingsbury, Kelsie B. Harder. <u>A Dictionary of American proverbs</u>. Oxford: Oxford University Press, 1992.

Yates, Norris Wilson. <u>Robert Benchley</u>. Ann Arbor: University of Michigan, 1968.

Appendix C: Endnotes

Part 1, Chapter 1

[1] Endodontic (root canal) training class.

[2] Discretionary time added on by the referee in a soccer match for injuries and stoppages at the end of regulation time after the first half and at the match's end.

Part 1, Chapter 2

[3] Brian Kakuk - bahamasunderground.com, Steve Bogaerts – aztecdiving. com and Paul Heinerth http://www.iantd.com/ (see instructor listings).

[4] The Columbia River forms the border between much of Oregon and Washington.

Part 1, Chapter 4

[5] Dimitar Berbatov, a Bulgarian international player, plays his club football for Manchester United.

[6] "Pitch" is a term used by Brits and Australians to describe a sporting field.

[7] Football has an enduring appeal, history and tradition both on and off the pitch. Football teams do not move from one city to another. Aston Villa from Birmingham in the English midlands of the English Premier League, for example, will never move to Newcastle in the northeast of England. This permanence, in part, helps cement the bond between football clubs and their supporters. In addition, across the globe, teams tangibly bring to life both the desperation and aspirations of their supporters at the local club level as well as on the international stage. The outpouring of well-earned pride in Germany after the 2006 World Cup provides a glimpse of this. Over 500,000 people came to the Brandenburg Gate in Berlin after the tournament to celebrate the achievements of the German national team. (German fans thank team in mass celebration) Not expected to do much at the start of the tournament, the team finished third under their new coach Juergen Klinsmann, a World Cup winner and player with Germany at Italia '90. (Klinnsman Pays Tribute to Players) What made the team's achievement all the more remarkable was that this was Klinsmann's first top level job in soccer management. (Whiteside) It is virtually unheard of to have a national team manager appointed without professional coaching

experience. Klinsmann and his team lifted the entire country. On that day in Berlin, vast seas of German flags and clothing carrying the national colors washed over the celebration. Such a positive display of nationalism and unity had not been seen in Germany since the fall of the Berlin Wall.

Other examples abound. For example, Barcelona FC is the pride of the Catalan region of Spain. Abuses to the Catalan people during the Spanish Civil war in 1936-39 created a palpable animosity between the Castilians of Madrid and the Catalans of Barcelona. (Wikes) The hated nemesis of Barcelona FC is none other than the "Royal Whites," the Madridistas, Real Madrid.

Boca Juniors in Buenos Aires is a club steeped deeply in the history of the local working class and is an immense source of pride for its supporters. Their fierce rivals, River Plate, are generally considered better heeled. Derby matches between the two are among the fiercest on the planet and are a classic exhibition of the struggle for respect between the haves and have-nots. (Hamilton)

Glasgow Celtic and Glasgow Rangers have a similar animosity and rivalry based on traditional religious affiliations. In the 19th century, there was an upsurge in emigration due to the potato famine from Ireland to the United States, Canada and especially Scotland, where over 300,000 Irish emigrated. (Shannon) The majority of these Irish immigrants were Catholic. Celtic was founded in 1887 as a charity to help alleviate the poverty many of these Irish immigrants. (Old Firm's enduring appeal) Rangers was established by the Protestant majority within Glasgow and until 1989 notoriously refused to sign Catholic players. (Old Firm's enduring appeal) In addition to the political and social factors that make their tension so strong, one of these two teams or the other has dominated Scottish football over the past 50 years.

Without the traditions above, with all due respect, it is difficult to envision such passion ever being displayed over the results of the LA Clippers (NBA), Nashville Predators (NHL), Baltimore Orioles (MLB) or the Houston Texans (NFL). Part of what fuels this lack of fervor in some corners of American professional sports is the automatic inclusion in our leagues. If the teams do poorly one year, they compete in the same league the next year without consequence. This is not the case in any major football league in the world. When a team finishes at the bottom of the table they are "relegated." When relegated, the team moves to the next lower division and the champions of the lower division are "promoted" to the higher level. (Premier League Handbook 2008/09: Rules) This raises the quality and fierceness of competition across the entire league structure.

The financial consequences of relegation are dire. In England for example, tens of millions of British pounds are lost when a team is relegated. The investment in time, energy and money to gain promotion back into the Promised Land of the English Premier League is substantial, if it is possible. One cannot buy success on a football pitch. Some teams never recover. Queens Park Rangers (QPR), for example, was relegated from the top flight of English football and has languished in the lower divisions catastrophically ever since (A potted history of QPR 1882-2009) and recently flirted with bankruptcy. (Hale)

Teams at the top of the league are playing both for the league championship and the right to play in larger regional and global competitions. For example, the top four teams in England are entered into what is known as the "UEFA Champions League" where they will play similar high finishing teams from around Europe. Eventually this tournament yields a "Champion" of Europe with monstrous financial incentives.

8 It is noteworthy that Manchester, England, also has a blue half. Ironically, the divisions in Manchester are as palpable as the red and blue division to American politics. The blue half is graced by Manchester City, a team that since the 1992-93 season has both been relegated and promoted and never finished higher than 8th in the English Premier League. (Smith)

The pride of the red half of Manchester is understandable. Coincident to the formation of the English premier league in 1992, Man Yoo began to emerge as winners and have dominated the top tier of English football up to the present day. Globally, only two football teams, AC Milan and Real Madrid, have records that in this period rival or possibly surpass them. Man Yoo's honors include: 11 Premier League titles: 92/93, 93/94, 95/96, 96/97, 98/99, 99/00, 00/01, 02/03, 06/07, 07/08 and 08/09. They have never finished lower than third place since the inception of the English Premier league. They have come in second place three times, and third place three times, won the European Championship twice in 98/99 and 07/08, the FA Cup four times in 93/94, 94/95, 98/99 and 03/04, the League Cup two times in 1992 and 2006, the Intercontinental cup once in 1999 and the FIFA Club World Cup once in 2008. (The club since 1878)

In addition, Cristiano Ronaldo won the Ballon d'Or in 2008 (European Footballer of the Year) and the European Golden Shoe in 2008 (31 goals). In 2008, Cristiano Ronaldo was named the FIFA World Player of the Year. (White) In 1999, David Beckham was the UEFA Player of the Year. (UEFA Club Football Awards)

Manchester United is consistently ranked as one of the richest clubs in the world based on annual financial turnover and has been so since the establishment of the English Premier League in 1992. (Real top Man Utd in rich league) Virtually every match is a sellout of over 75,000. The majority of fans have paid for the rights to purchase tickets through a membership club. Every week there are thousands of fans unable to get tickets. (James) A recent Google search for Manchester United yielded over 60 million entries. (July 2009) Man Yoo supporters are proud and possessive of their team. For example, when American owners purchased Man Yoo in 2005, there were small riots in Manchester and large crowds of protesters. (Glazer wins control of Man United) The message was clear: this is our game, our heritage, Yankee go home. Such protest has died completely given their recent dominance of English football.

[9] Sir Alex Ferguson has been the Man Yoo manager (coach) since November 1986. (Sir Alex Ferguson) When one considers how quickly managers come and go in English football at the highest level, with some being fired in as few as eight matches, this is a remarkable achievement, as some teams play as many as 60 to 70 matches in a single season. (Davies) Ferguson's long-term record is among the very best in world sport. He was named the "Most Influential Man in British Sport" by the Times newspaper in January 2009. (Slot) Man Yoo fans around the world hang on his every word, not unlike how the financial markets await the word of the chairman of the United States Federal Reserve. Fans want to know of possible transfer targets (players the club wants to buy) and which are surplus to the requirements and may be sold. They want to know of injuries, the expected dates for a player's return or to get his assessment of a given performance, trend or the opposition. With very few exceptions, Sir Alex has an impeccable record for knowing when to sell players at their peak (David Beckham) who then lose form and never regain their once pre-eminent status. While not all expensive transfers into the club have panned out well (José Kléberson, Juan Veron), some of the talent purchased at modest rates have been extremely good buys in relation both to their contributions to the team (Christiano Ronaldo, Roy Keane, Eric Cantona) and to their financial value when they were sold. (Solhekol) The youth system at Man Yoo is ultimately overseen by Sir Alex and produced an unprecedented series of international class players in the mid 1990s (Nicky Butt, David Beckham, Ryan Giggs, Gary Neville, Philip Neville, Paul Scholes). (Wallace)

"Fergie," as Sir Alex Ferguson is affectionately known, is famous for his "hair dryer" treatment of players who do not perform. It is widely rumored that a cut received under David Beckham's eye may have involved a well-placed kick of a boot in the Man Yoo dressing room. (Beckham forgives Ferguson) He is famously intolerant of not only underperformance but also insubordination. It is Fergie's way or the highway. Big football names like

Gabriel Heinze, Ruud Van Nistelrooy and Japp Stam, to name a few, have come and gone at Old Trafford because they would not tow his line.

He is a master of the "mind games" played with opposing managers. Kevin Keegan, the manager of Newcastle United in the 1995-1996 season, for example, lost the plot and went mildly cuckoo during a televised interview in response to Fergie's verbal jousting. To this day, a diehard English football supporter hearing the words "I would luuuv it if we beat them" immediately brings flooding back the memory of Keegan forgetting that the game is played on the pitch and not between the manager's ears. Man Yoo went on to win the championship that year. Kevin Keegan and Newcastle finished second. (Premier League History: Season 1995/96) Sir Alex Ferguson and Arsene Wenger (the manager of Arsenal) have also engaged in their share of mind games over their respective managerial tenures.

[10] Despite my bleeding the Red colors of Man Yoo, my true spiritual football home is actually Tottenham Hotspur (Spurs), a North London club with a storied tradition that has had relatively little success since the inception of the English Premier league in 1992-1993. (A History of The Premier League) Perhaps like a suitor that lost interest, in time, Spurs lost mine.

[11] While women's soccer is immensely popular in the United States, especially at a competitive youth and collegiate level, professionally, outside America, this is a game followed in large measure by men. Men, while they would probably never admit it, love the game for all the things that happen off the pitch as much as the things that happen on it. Men do not need soap operas, gossip magazines or drama in their movies; they have a planet for this unto themselves, "Planet Football." (Drama Across Planet Football) The world of the round ball and all its trappings are the ultimate in live, unpredictable and very public theatrical improvisation. An apt description, Old Trafford, the home ground of Man Yoo, is known as the "theatre of dreams." (Westwood) Planet Football is a spectacle played out on a global stage. Little about teams, players and what happens from the boardroom to the locker room ever stays truly private. In the shadows, there are agents, manufacturers, and vast commercial interests in the form of betting syndicates, advertisers, sponsors and banks surrounding the game. At the end of the day, when the curtain rises, very little is left unrevealed to the public. Such is the incessant demand for more of everything about the footballing world: more access to the players, coaches and decision makers, in essence more back-story to create heroes and villains of the human beings who manage and play a game held dear by its supporters.

Part of football's appeal is that the in its small corner of the universe, all human triumph, tragedy, farce, satire, greed and sacrifice are personified in flesh and blood by 22 players (11 per team) trying to push a piece of leather past the opponent's goal line without their hands touching the ball excepting the two goalkeepers. This endeavor is played most commonly with the unspoken rule that whatever the referee does not call as foul is fair game. Within the larger match, smaller one-on-one skirmishes take place between opposing players. The result of most matches is ultimately determined by which team collectively wins these individual battles. For example, one team's right-winger (attacking player) will line up against the other's left defensive back. While nothing like man-on-man coverage in basketball, the more times the winger can get behind the defender and cross (kick) the ball into the center of the goal mouth the more likely goals will be scored. Over the 90 minutes of a game, there is little room for hiding. If your opposition is faster, stronger and more skilled, you will be found out and your weaknesses exposed. As a result, a certain degree of "nasty" behavior takes place in the form of shirt pulling, trash talking and ankle clipping, among other forms of skullduggery. Such equalizing tactics, hopefully unseen by the referee, can go far to neutralize the advantages of your opponent.

[12] There is usually a knife-edge to English football matches of one kind or another. Whether a relegation battle, a fight for the league title, a local derby (a match played by two teams from the same city), or possibly to determine who will qualify for European tournaments. In addition to the above, these matches are a tangible manifestation of the struggles of conflicting groups ignited on any one of a number of different fuses alluded to before, including hooliganism.

Hooligans participate in disruptive or unruly behavior around football matches. Organized hooligans traditionally belonged to "firms" intent on violence. Most hooligan behavior is committed in public places. Traditionally, firms have used football matches as an excuse to get drunk and violent and give voice to their dissatisfaction with the status quo. Unemployed, with time on their hands, football has been a magnet for the disaffected and an easy target on which to focus frustrations.

To this day, there are riot police on horseback outside English matches on call for crowd disturbances. The tragedy at Sheffield United's Hillsborough stadium in 1989 was a watershed. Although not directly related to hooligan behavior, it demonstrates the need for such police presence. Ninety-three people were killed and more than 200 others injured during a crowd surge where fans were apparently let into the ground without tickets. (1989: Football fans crushed at Hillsborough)

Decades of violent incidents and riots between rival firms (such as the infamous Chelsea Headhunters, Leeds United Service Crew and Birmingham

Zulus) (Spaaij) and the Hillsborough disaster led to reform. The Taylor Report, published in January 1990, was an inquiry set up by the Home Office (a British governmental department that addresses immigration and crime) to study the problem and make recommendations. The Taylor Report, a direct result of the Hillsborough disaster and hooliganism mandated "all seater" stadiums in the top tier of English football, among many other changes. (Taylor)

The line between hooligan and supporter is not an altogether clear one. The elements needed to make an otherwise good natured match day combust into violence are a mixture of alcohol, overcrowding and opposing fans meeting (on purpose or by accident) after an especially contentious match. These combinations blended with perceived, current or past insults are incendiary.

While one step removed from domestic English football, the violent history of England fans outside of the British Isles has been especially gruesome, as exemplified by the deaths of 39 people and injury to 600 others in Heysel, Belgium, in May, 1985 in the European Cup final between the Italian team Juventus FC and Liverpool FC. (The Heysel disaster) English supporters charged the Italian supporters and in their retreat a retaining wall collapsed, leading to the majority of deaths and injuries. English clubs were subsequently banned entirely from European competitions for five years. (1985: Uefa bans English clubs from Europe) In the present era, though, domestic English football matches have been largely cleaned up from organized hooliganism, although now much of the violence occurs away from the stadium itself.

[13] Daft is a "Briticism" meaning stupid or silly.

[14] The Stretford end of Old Trafford is the one closest to the tunnel leading to the pitch.

[15] "Kyboshed" means to stop, veto or put an end to something.

[16] Unguarded.

[17] The "table" is the British term for the league standings.

[18] To be illegally recruited.

[19] To "slag someone off" is to hurl a series of insults or criticisms.

[20] Ironically, the world football supporter is starved for almost any such news in the American domestic media. By contrast, football coverage elsewhere in

the world is exhaustive. With fanzines, official club magazines, membership clubs, e-newsletters, text alerts, match day programs, a bewildering array of Internet sites in addition to the matches themselves (live and televised), there are an infinite number of ways for supporters to stay connected with their team. Top-level players and managers cannot step outside their doors without paparazzi. Small forests were cut down to supply the paper needed to report on the rumored transfer of Cristiano Ronaldo from Manchester United to Real Madrid in the summer of 2008. (Queiroz urges Ronaldo to stay put) Even though there was not much to the story at the time and Ronaldo was not transferred, weeks of mounting speculation had fans outside of the United States, wanting to know if the world player of the year for the 2007-2008 season was changing clubs. (Queiroz urges Ronaldo to stay put) Cristiano Ronaldo, much like Sir Alex Ferguson, could walk down any street in the United States without being recognized, except probably by everyone from any other part of the globe. On June 11, 2009, Ronaldo was transferred from Manchester United to Real Madrid for a staggering world record transfer fee of £80 million ($132 million). (Ogden)

[21] These stories rival in substance and style even the most compelling television dramas.

[22] Football has its own language. Once learned, this language can easily sort the true football "supporter" from a wannabe. "Fans" push air around on hot days; "supporters" eat drink and sleep their teams. In a post-match interview, if a player says, "We done the business" it means, "It was ugly, but we won and that is what matters." When one team dominates another, it is known as a "hiding." It is "meat and drink" to supply a striker with opportunities that they can easily score from. Intelligence in soccer is known as having a good "football brain." Having the athleticism to be as competitive late in the match as one was in the early going is known as having an "engine." The dictionary of such terms is extensive.

[23] Being American does not absolve me of responsibility for my tribal loyalty to Man Yoo. In fact, it compounds a crime in the eyes of my English friends who believe that I should support Arsenal, Liverpool and other English Football clubs.

[24] The home of Arsenal Football Club before they moved to The Emirates, their new stadium, in 2006.

[25] Man Yoo midfielder.

[26] Arsenal midfielder.

[27] Man Yoo defender.

Part 1, Chapter 5

[28] A place for couples to "neck."

[29] "Briticism" for a night out on the town consuming mass quantities of alcohol.

[30] Entrance exam for medical school in the United States.

[31] Football legends. Georgie Best is George Best, Zizou is Zinedine Zidane, Puskas is Fernec Puskas and Distefano is Alfredo Di Stefano.

[32] National stadium of England. Two years overdue and an estimated £400 or $650 million over budget, Wembley was rebuilt and completed in 2007. (Power)

[33] Soccer parlance: to score a goal from very little, making something happen out of nothing.

[34] Walter Mitty was a character in The Secret life of Walter Mitty by James Thurber. Walter often daydreams of secret plans or fascinating adventures while living a tedious and dull life in reality. (Walter Mitty)

[35] Diego Maradona is considered to be one of the most talented footballers of all time. He is most famous for his 1986 goal against England in the World Cup, where over 60 meters he weaved between six different England players and scored. His goal was voted by FIFA (Federal International Football Association) as the "'goal of the century." (Diego Maradona goal voted the FIFA World Cup™ Goal of the Century)

[36] During a football match, a yellow card is a warning or caution card given to a player for, among other infractions, an offence that could injure another player. If a player receives two yellow cards in one match, they are given a red card and sent off the pitch. A straight red card is given to a player who commits a foul that could cause serious injury. After receiving a red card, the player's team must play shorthanded for the rest of the match.

[37] American novelists. Richard Ford is most famous for his book The Sportswriter. Peter Dexter is most famous for his novel Paris Trout.

[38] Jean-Michel Basquiat is a famous American painter from New York (1960-1988) and known for his neo-expressionist art. The Dutch Masters were a group of painters from the Dutch Golden Age of painting (1584-1702). They are especially highly regarded in part, for their mastery in the use of light. Their ranks included Johannes Vermeer van Delft and Rembrandt

Harmenszoon van Rijn.

[39] Highly rated California cabernet wines.

[40] Greek Islands known for their cultural significance and natural beauty.

[41] Nigirisushi is a type of sushi characterized by fish bound to a portion of rice by a thin piece of nori (seaweed). While there are many kinds of makisushi, this variety is generally rolled sushi that is held together circumferentially by a strip of nori. Sashimi is thinly sliced fresh fish served raw.

[42] A tea with proven health benefits typically served in Argentina, but popular in many Latin American countries.

Part 2

[43] "Jaws of Life" is a song on James McMurtry's album It Had to Happen. (James McMurty, It Had to Happen, 1997)

[44] Brian DesRoches MA, PhD is a prominent psychotherapist in Seattle, Washington.

[45] A soccer metaphor, this describes an aggressive, dangerous and often violent attempt to get the ball from another player without regard for their safety.

[46] A soccer reference; a match is 90 minutes long.

[47] Captain Bligh is famous for his command of the HMS Bounty. His crew began their journey from Portsmouth, England on December 23, 1787 to bring Tahitian breadfruit to the British colonies. The Bounty first stopped in Tenerife and then sailed to Cape Horn only to be met with violent storms. The crew's ability to survive the storms was, in part, due to Bligh's strict health and nutrition regime but also his approach to discipline. On October 26, 1788, the Bounty reached Matavai Bay, Tahiti. Upon leaving Tahiti, amid rising tensions, his crew began to fragment. On April 28, 1789, Fletcher Christian, acting lieutenant and second in command, led a mutiny against Bligh. Bligh was cast adrift along with 19 crewmembers. (The Mutiny on HMS Bounty) Christian took the HMS Bounty to Pitcairn Island; a significant navigational feat in its own right, by traveling 2,000 miles with incorrectly charted maps. Bligh even more remarkably reached Timor, Indonesia, traveling over 3,600 miles without navigational tools in an open launch. (Captain William Bligh)

[48] Easter Island is a living symbol of ecological devastation. When Europeans

first discovered Easter Island, it appeared to be uninhabitable.

[49] A phenomenon that people with general good merit and excellent accomplishment are criticized or resented because their talents distinguish them from others.

[50] Manchester United fans know Eric Cantona as "King Eric." Eric Cantona is one of the most gifted and enigmatic French footballers of all time and Manchester United's Player of the 20th century. (Spanton) Although Cantona is French, his fame primarily stemmed from his time in English football. (The Life and Times of Eric Cantona) He is infamously known for kung fu kicking a Crystal Palace fan during a 1995 match and calling Henri Michael, the coach of the French national team a "bag of shit" in an interview. He was banned from international duty but subsequently recalled. (1995: Cantona banned over attack on fan)

Part 3, Chapter 1

[51] Lhotse and Nuptse are both adjacent mountains to Mt. Everest.

Part 3, Chapter 5

[52] While no subject should be off limits, it is not necessary to regurgitate every past detail of who slept with whom, when and how, unless specifically asked. There is information that should be transmitted and that which should be left buried. What should be communicated might include anything that poses a health risk to the sexual union, or anything that has a direct bearing on the couple's future marriage out of bed. Other than this, if it will not unite the couple it should be left unspoken. This said, ask whatever you need to know. Yet be careful what you ask for. Once disclosed, for a marriage to have any hope of survival, the receiver of the information must be compassionate, understanding and forgiving. Otherwise, what is related may forge an indelible impression.

[53] A system of yoga that focuses on breathing and movement.

[54] K2 is part of the Karakoram Region stretching from Afghanistan to Kashmir. It is one of the highest mountain ranges in the world with its highest peak, K2, at 28,251 feet. (Karakoram Range)

[55] Guantanamo Bay, Cuba, is the location of the Guantanamo Bay Detention Camp operated by the United States government. Since opening in 2002, the camp has been riddled with controversy over the treatment of its detain-

ees as released prisoners made accusations of torture, sleep deprivation and sexual and cultural degradation. Many prisoners under an executive order signed by President George Bush in 2001 were detained for an indefinite time if considered a participant in international terror. In 2009, President Barack Obama signed an executive order to close the detention center by 2010.

Appendix A: The Q&A: "The Overhead Environment."

[56] Considered about 1.8 million years before our present time, the Pleistocene epoch is the third division of the geological time scale. (Pleistocene Epoch) During this time, most of the earth was covered with thick sheets of ice that changed the landscape of the earth, but towards the end of the Pleistocene epoch, the sheets of ice retreated and humans first appeared. (Pleistocene Epoch)

[57] Former U.S . Navy Diver, Brian Kakuk is a renowned cave guide, instructor and explorer living and working in Marsh Harbor, Abacos, Bahamas.

[58] The SS Andrea Doria was an Italian ocean liner that sank in 1956 by colliding with the Swedish American ship the MS Stockholm. It is considered the "Mt. Everest of technical wreck diving."

[59] Cave divers observe the "rule of thirds." One third of their gas supply is used going into the cave, one third to exit and the remaining third is reserved for emergencies.

[60] A "rebreather" is a closed circuit breathing system that provides oxygen to the diver while removing as much CO_2 as possible from the exhaled gas through "scrubbing" with a carbon dioxide absorbent.

[61] The more nitrogen that dissolves in the diver's bloodstream during a dive due to increasing pressure at greater depths, the more critical the requirement to "off gas" this nitrogen during ascent. Off gassing is known as "decompression." Beyond empirically derived "safe" limits, which do not require decompression, the diver has a "decompression obligation." The diver must modify their rate of ascent to exhale the excess dissolved nitrogen. Detailed tables and/or dive computers tell divers their "deco" time. Decompression stops range in number and length of time depending on the dive profile (maximum depth, dive time and gas mixtures used).

Open water recreational diving is based on the concept that the diver will not need to modify their ascent to remove the excess nitrogen that has been absorbed in the bloodstream. This is known as "no decompression diving." This term is a misnomer. All dives in fact are decompression dives to the extent that the diver is off gassing absorbed nitrogen upon ascending irrespective of the dive profile. For the purposes of clarity, the distinction between decompression diving and no decompression diving lies in the intentional stops that must be made in decompression diving rather than the lack of such stops in no decompression diving (aside from a short and arbitrary "safety" stop at 15 feet for three minutes taken as a precaution in the latter). If the diver ascends without off gassing as required for the dive profile, the gas comes out of solution in the bloodstream in the form of bubbles. Depending on the severity of the occurrence, symptoms can range from mild to fatal. (Kevin Gurr)

[62] PO2 is an abbreviation for the partial pressure of a gas within a fluid. In this case, oxygen in blood. A correct PO2 provides adequate oxygen saturation in the bloodstream. Low PO2 causes blackout, as may occur at high altitudes. High PO2 causes oxygen toxicity, manifested, in part, as convulsions for divers. Monitoring PO2 at all times underwater is a standard safeguard in technical diving. (Kevin Gurr)